HURRICANE KITCHEN

HURRICANE KITCHEN

How to Cook Healthy Foods
for Large Groups and Institutions

RICK PERRY

Illustrations by Douglas Alvord

An earlier version of this work, entitled
The Integration of Natural Foods in an Institutional Setting,
was copyrighted in 1985 by Rick Perry Ink.

Designed by John O'Brien.
Cover photo by Rick Perry.

Appreciation is expressed to the Hurricane Island Outward Bound School in Rockland, Maine, for its cooperation in the production of this book.

When recipes in the book are referred to, they have initial capital letters and are italicized.

Printed in the United States of America.

Library of Congress Cataloging-in-Publication Data
Perry, Rick.
    Hurricane kitchen.
    Includes index.
    1. Quantity cookery.   2. Cookery (Natural foods)
I. Title.
TX820.P34 1988   641.5'7   87-26683
ISBN 0-912769-12-2

Second printing

Dedication

to those cooks who have realized the need to change
the American diet

Contents

PART I: Starting to use natural foods in large-scale menus

1. Introduction

Food for body and soul 10
Grains — the key to a balanced diet 12

2. Menu planning

Fresh, real foods 16
The simplest meal of all 17
Pasta-based meals 19
Main meal suggestions 20
Lunch menus 22
Presentation and mechanics of serving 26
Cost effectiveness 28
Managing leftovers 30
Taste 31

3. Real foods

Whole grains 32
The amazing soybean 36
Legumes 37
Oil 38
Sweeteners 40
Red meat 40
Seaweeds 41
Yogurt 42
Spices 43
Beverages 44

4. Kitchen equipment 46

5. Ordering staples and setting up a grain room 52

Part II: The recipes: preparing basic whole foods

1. Whole-grain recipes 56
    Breakfast Foods 58
    Lunch and Dinner.....................................67
    Homemade Pasta 68
2. Breads and other baked goods 72
    Yeast Breads 73
    Unleavened Breads 86
3. Quick breads 90
4. Pancakes, crepes and pie crusts 98
5. Soups...104
6. Real food for main meals 110
    Cooking Beans and Other Legumes.....................110
    Cooking Seaweeds 115
    Baking Whole Foods 116
    Sautéing Vegetables 118
7. Main dishes 120
8. Salads and dressings.................................136
9. Gravies and sauces 142
10. Spreads, dips, yogurt, alternative beverages...........150
11. Desserts 154
About Outward Bound 164
About the author 164
Books of interest 165
Index 166
Acknowledgement 172

PART I

Starting to use natural foods in large-scale menus

1. Introduction

Food for body and soul

FOR TWELVE YEARS I have run the kitchen at Hurricane Island Outward Bound School off the coast of Maine. A very special place where people can start to transform their lives, Hurricane Island has been an ideal location in which to develop a healthy-foods diet for large groups that is practical, palatable, economical, and flexible.

From the beginning of my career as an institutional cook, I have used a "transitional approach." That is, I try gently to integrate whole, healthy foods into people's diets — rather than have them abandon all their eating habits and preferences at once. This has worked well for most people unfamiliar with whole foods, from day-care children to senior citizens.

Whole grains provide about half the bulk of our Hurricane Island diet, and the remainder is a balanced variety of fresh fruits and vegetables, legumes, dairy products, and fresh fish. Chicken is offered weekly, red meat rarely.

My nutritional convictions have grown from personal experience. I am a cook, not a doctor. Because this is essentially a workbook for cooks, medical evidence and research data have no place here. There are many excellent books on the market that one can turn to for the hard facts on nutrition. (See the bibliography.) I am not a health-food evangelist nor a macrobiotic extremist — although much of what I have learned about dietary balance has come from Michio Kushi's macrobiotic theories. I simply believe that people require whole foods — real foods — to be as healthy and as happy as they can be. I assume that the reader/cook accepts this, so the preaching in this book is brief.

Let me just remind you of this: Food is not only fuel for our bodies, it is also what builds them and keeps our mental and emotional beings healthy and well balanced. Muscle tone, keen vision, healthy hair, clear skin, and general vitality are the outer manifestations of a health-giving diet. The ability to think clearly, concentrate, cope with life's challenges, attain peace of mind and success in one's work, and to maintain positive emotional relationships with people are its inner fruits.

Our bodies are the product of millions of years of evolution. During that evolution, humans consumed foods that the environment provided. These foods were naturally occurring and unadulterated. Evolution, in concert with those foods, created and designed our bodies. It is unreasonable to expect our bodies to function properly with food that no longer even remotely resembles the foods we were designed to eat.

Is anyone surprised that our hospitals are full? There is no way we can cheat our bodies of the nutrients they need without paying a high price. Degenerative diseases, cancer, diabetes, mental illness are rampant in our culture, and the connection between these ills and our diet has been well established.

Healthy people live joyful and peaceful lives. Those who abuse their health become aggressive, depressed, discontented, or ill in other ways. Whenever you shop for food, go out to eat, or take any substance into your body, you make a decision that determines the quality of your life. You are free to choose a diet and a way of life that allows your whole being to function properly rather than passively to accept a life that is detrimental to body, mind, and spirit. When you decide to improve the quality of your life, diet is a natural place to begin.

Healthy cooks make healthy food — and literally make healthy people who eat the food. Food prepared with love and joy nourish those who eat it on a deeper level than protein and vitamins. This seems obvious in a family situation, but it is equally true when you are cooking for scores of people. When you are selected to cook for a group, you become a leader. You have the power to improve the physical and mental health of everyone you serve. If you cook with love and joy, you can experience your position as a cook as one of great influence — not of drudgery. Your power as a cook can be a healing power.

Grains – the key to a balanced diet

FOR THOUSANDS OF YEARS mankind has depended on grains as the primary diet staple. It is hardly surprising that nutritionists agree that you must include a substantial amount of whole grains in your diet for optimum health. This does not mean exchanging tasty foods for plain, unpalatable "health foods." Not at all! Every favorite food — if it is real food — can be included in a grain-based diet.

Grains, which are both a seed and a fruit, are balanced whole foods containing proteins, carbohydrates, fats, vitamins, and minerals. "Give us this day our daily bread" has a universal significance. Throughout history, indigenous grains have been used by local cultures: corn in the Americas, rice in Asia, millet in the Near East, wheat in Europe. The early American settlers based their diet on oats, wheat, and barley, eating roughly fifty percent grains and less than ten percent meat. In this century, that proportion has been reversed. What is more, the grain products most Americans consume today have been devitalized by modern processing and milling methods.

A high-protein, high-fat diet used to symbolize affluence, just as did refined flour and refined sugar. This has resulted in the average American now consuming two hundred and twenty pounds of meat, one hundred and ten pounds of sugar, and less than ten pounds of whole grains per person per year. I hope that the transitional menus and recipes offered in this cookbook will help many to bridge the gap these statistics show.

2. Menu planning

IN PLANNING MENUS for a workable, transitional diet, the first thing I suggest is that you rely on fresh whole foods — real foods — to the greatest extent possible. When you offer foods from any part of the food spectrum, serve only the real thing. For example, if you are going to serve coffee in the morning, use freshly ground beans. Not only will it taste better, it will be less expensive! If serving meat, use fresh products from local farms, if possible.

The reason I recommend a transitional approach to healthy foods is that many people are discouraged or react very negatively when their diet is changed radically overnight. It is far better to weed out harmful foods gradually as you introduce healthier alternatives. This allows the body to keep pace with the modifications and to heal itself. It also gives the individual time to adjust mentally without a sense of deprivation.

The evening meal is a great place to start replacing refined grains and starches with the real thing. For example, look at your present menu and wherever you see potato, write grain. (I have nothing against potatoes, except that they show up much too often on institutional menus.) Replace stove-top stuffings and precooked rice with unprocessed whole grains.

If you are unfamiliar with whole grains, I suggest you start with simple combinations that I have found work well: brown rice with fish, millet with chicken, and whole-wheat pasta with just about any main dish. See the suggested menus for other specific combinations that have proved especially successful with diners new to whole foods. Grains are infinitely versatile. They can be served at lunch in the form of bread, muffins, or crackers. On hot days you might offer chilled whole-grain salad such as tabouli. In cold weather, leftover grains can round out hearty soups. And leftover grains can always be turned into delicious breads.

Hot and cold whole-grain cereals are breakfast basics. You can delight your school, camp, church, restaurant, daycare center, or whatever your community is with pancakes, muffins, or waffles made from freshly ground whole-grain flours. With skillful arrangement of five basic breakfast foods — eggs, quick-breads, french toast, hot and cold cereals — your diners need never be bored.

Breakfast menus can be varied endlessly by your selection of secondary foods — fresh and stewed fruits, yogurts, natural sweeteners, and beverages.

Fresh, real foods

IN THE CONVERSION to a healthy menu, the four areas that need the most work are:

1. Lack of whole grains and freshly ground flours.
2. Elimination of factory-packaged and preprocessed foods.
3. Lack of fresh vegetables.
4. Lack of alternative protein sources to red meat.

The most efficient way to integrate whole grains into the menu is to set up a system for your own bread production. It will also save you money. The most important ingredient in bread is the flour. You should start with flour freshly ground either in your own flour mill or purchased from a natural-food wholesaler. For groups of fifteen or more people, I strongly recommend investing in a flour mill. The mill will pay for itself in a relatively short time while giving you a variety of freshly ground flours and meals second to none in flavor and nutritional value. (For more detailed information about flour mills, see page 48.)

I have found that the key to successful food service is the quality of ingredients used. Many schools and camps have menus that look exactly the same as mine on paper. A typical summer-camp breakfast menu might look like this: toast with jam, home-fried potatoes, eggs, cereal, juice, fruit, tea, and coffee. However, the flavor and nutrition at that table would be vastly different from mine. Their toast would be white rather than the whole-wheat toast that I offer; they would use canned jelly rather than unrefined honey; the eggs they use might well have been stored in a warehouse for six months, whereas mine are farm fresh; their home-fried potatoes are factory-processed and frozen — mine are made from fresh potatoes. Every component of the menu is degraded by using seemingly cheaper and more convenient products which, in the long run, are *more* expensive, less nutritious, less appealing to the palate and eye, and, of course, ridden with chemical "enhancers" and preservatives, some of which are harmful.

It is fine to serve traditional American food, as long as it is real food. Start by replacing all packaged and processed items and prepare all your dishes from scratch with fresh ingredients. Invariably, you will find that you can come up with a better product for less money. The extra time involved in preparation will be offset by the lower expense of whole foods versus the factory products. It is always cheaper to make your own baked goods than to buy them, even if you have to hire an extra cook.

The question of alternative protein is the "meat" of the next section!

The simplest meal of all

AS YOU BEGIN PLANNING whole-foods menus, you will often find yourself relying on a combination of grain, vegetables, and legumes; for example, brown rice and sautéed vegetables with boiled kidney beans. Combining rice with beans yields a high-quality protein like meat has, with the essential amino acids in proper proportion. Grain by itself does not provide all the elements of complete protein. Rice also provides fiber, complex carbohydrates, and essential B vitamins. The vegetables provide other vitamins and minerals. I don't feel that it is necessary to compute the nutrients provided by every ingredient one serves, because most grain, vegetable, and bean combinations make nutritious meals. Some researchers feel that the nutritional intake of an entire day is what matters, not what

a single meal provides. In any case, a combination of grain, vegetable, and legume is the basic nutritious meal.

In planning a palatable meal of this type, consider the colors of the foods you are combining. For example, if you select golden millet, don't serve soybeans with it — bright red kidney beans would make the meal far more pleasing to the eye. Think in terms of contrast. It seems that when the colors on your plate are contrasting, the meal is likely to be nutritionally balanced. The examples I give of a grain-vegetable-legume meal are just a few of the many possibilities for a simple but appetizing menu. Note that in my menus adding gravy or sesame salt rounds out simple three-part meals in terms of both taste and nutrition.

An example of the basics:

Brown rice baked in vegetable broth seasoned with sesame seeds.
Aduki beans simmered with onions and garlic, seasoned with tamari and black pepper.
Vegetable such as a mixture of sautéed red and white onions, broccoli, mushrooms, red peppers, and snow peas.
The garnishes
Gravy such as yeast gravy — my favorite — or bechamel or miso-tahini sauce.
Seaweed such as arame, cooked with onion and carrot slivers, served with a sprinkling of finely chopped chives and a touch of broth.

Each component of this basic meal can be varied, providing an unlimited array of simple but complete meals. For example, one might replace the brown rice with barley, bulgur, kasha, or millet. One can also serve the grain in many different forms: fried, baked, or boiled, or in dishes such as grilled millet patties or other grain burgers. There are many legumes to choose from — kidney, black, pinto, garbanzo (chickpea), aduki (azuki), cattle, navy, or lima beans; or green or yellow peas, whole or split. Let taste, color, and texture guide your selection.

For vegetables, we do best to rely on what is available at any given time of year in our locale. Here in the northeast we eat many root vegetables in the winter, because they are easiest to obtain then. But as things warm up, leafy green, tender, perishable vegetables become available and are a welcome change.

Gravy is always optional, but I find it very helpful for people new to whole foods who may miss meat and potato dinners; using it is part of the transitional approach.

The variety of seaweed you serve will depend upon what you can obtain locally. Natural-food stores and wholesalers now stock several different types of dried sea vegetables. Try serving bancha-twig tea with this basic meal; it seems to go well with it.

Pasta-based meals

Pasta

You can choose from ramen, soba, udon, artichoke, or homemade pasta. Use red sauce rarely as most Oriental and homemade noodles are too delicate for the traditional Italian tomato sauce. I prefer lightly dressing them with olive oil or mushrooms sautéed in oil along with sprinklings of freshly grated black pepper and parmesan cheese.

Protein

Incorporate fish or other seafood such as shrimp, scallops, or clams, sautéed in oil, or a soy protein food such as tofu or tempeh.

Vegetable

Select fresh local vegetables and/or salad greens to complement the protein and pasta in terms of color; for example, white fish with brown pasta and a green vegetable or salad.

Main meal suggestions

THE FOLLOWING ARE EXAMPLES of well-rounded meals that will help your diners make the transition to a natural-foods diet. Note that many include dishes that are familiar to the average American. Remember, the idea is to incorporate real foods in forms acceptable to most people while eliminating other ones gradually.

In your own planning, remember to use whole grains often and to combine them with legumes for maximum protein yields. In the following sample menus, note that red meat does not appear at all; chicken appears only once, fish twice, and quiche is the only dairy-based main dish. The fats here are very thin!

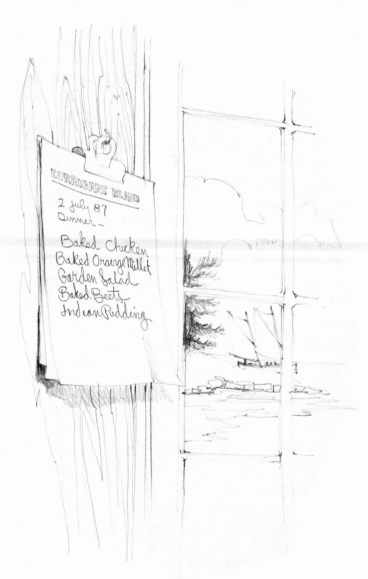

Sample Menus

1. Baked brown rice
   Sautéed vegetables –
      toasted sesame oil
   Aduki beans
   Baked tofu
   Yeast gravy

2. Baked chicken
   Baked orange millet
   Garden salad – French dressing
   Baked beets – soy mayonnaise
   Dessert (optional)

3. Baked fish
   Baked bulgur/kasha
   Garden salad –
      orange tahini dressing
   Fruit dessert

4. Fried tempeh
   Kidney beans –
      cooked with apple and onions
   Baked vegetables – mixed
   Baked grain
   Bechamel sauce

5. Italian-style spaghetti
   Traditional spaghetti sauce
   Steamed broccoli – parmesan cheese
   French/Italian bread – garlic butter
   Basic Italian salad

6. Mushroom and onion quiche
   Garden salad – French dressing
   Ramen noodles in tamari broth
   Baked vegetables

7. Lentil/rice stew
   Unleavened cereal bread
   Salad or coleslaw

8. Seitan – breaded and grilled
   Baked kasha
   Baked parsnips/onions/carrots
   Miso tahini gravy

9. Mexican refried beans
   Salsa
   Fresh whole-wheat tortillas
   Assorted fillers: chopped lettuce,
      black olives, diced vegetables,
      grated cheese, yogurt,
      fresh diced tomatoes

10. Fish chowder
    Custard corn bread
    Coleslaw
    Crackers – whole-wheat

11. Ratatouille with parmesan cheese
    Grain or pasta
    Green salad

12. Vegetable tempura
    Soba noodles in broth
    Grilled tofu
    Hijiki sea vegetable
    Ginger tamari sauce
       (for dipping tempura)
    Tempura apple and banana slices
       (for dessert)

Lunch menus

1. Soup, salad and bread

Soup is easy to prepare, given a few basic techniques. More often than not, I add leftover grains and vegetables to whatever broth I have on hand. Leftover beans or sea vegetables yield a rich, flavorful broth. Soups are economical and offer high-quality nutrition. In larger dining halls equipped with steam tables, soups are a perfect choice for lunch. Salad can vary from light summer greens to a hearty combination of raw vegetables with cubed cheese or tofu. Salads work well for large groups if someone monitors the salad bar so that it doesn't get too messy and doesn't run out of vital ingredients. The breads served at a soup and salad lunch should be hearty and nutritious since they constitute a major portion of the nutrition. I usually offer a variety of whole-grain breads: thinly sliced unleavened, basic whole-wheat, rye, and so on.

There are endless variations on this theme:

- Split pea soup
- Mushroom miso soup
- Black bean soup
- Chili
- Corn chowder
- Vegetable minestrone
- Cream of broccoli
- Lentil barley stew
- French onion (miso-base) soup

- Corn bread
- Unleavened rice bread
- Tortillas
- Custard corn bread
- Whole-wheat sesame crackers
- Whole-wheat Italian bread
- Fresh scones
- Wheat/oat crackers
- Whole-wheat croutons

2. Sandwich ideas

Americans tend to rely on sandwiches for lunch. There are many healthful ways to keep from boring everyone with the usual fare. Here are a few alternatives that have been well received at Hurricane Island.

The possibilities are endless!

Sandwich suggestions

- Seitan with sauerkraut, mustard, and melted Swiss cheese

- Hummus, avocado, and tomato on a bed of lettuce

- Fresh peanut butter with banana slices

- Tortillas with refried beans, hot sauce, and diced vegetables

- Sautéed vegetables with cheese on whole-wheat toast

- Cream cheese and olives on rye bread

- Soysage burgers on whole-wheat rolls with lettuce and tomato

- Fried tofu cake with lettuce, tomato, and soy mayonnaise

Presentation and mechanics of serving

KEEP IT SIMPLE! Be aware of color, texture, temperature, consistency, contrasts, and complement. One sprig of parsley can visually control a big bowl of rice.

One of a cook's big tasks is to get the food from kitchen to table without loss of quality. Ideally, hot foods should still be hot; and cold foods, cold. Pasta must not be mushy nor should salads be limp. All these and a myriad of other requirements of presentation and serving are challenges to professional cooks. Natural foods can be presented successfully to every group you serve.

The two most common methods of serving food to large gatherings are cafeteria-style and family-style. Both have their advantages and drawbacks. The advantages of having people queue for cafeteria service increase proportionately to the numbers served. If your steam table can be properly monitored and stocked, it can be very successful, but if not maintained correctly it can be disastrous. The secret lies in predicting the flow of traffic and cooking the necessary amounts of food at the proper time so that everything is ready when needed.

Family-style, or buffet-style, is often used for groups of less than two hundred and can work very well. Family-style serving encourages sharing at the table as well as giving the diner a sense of participation in the creation of his or her own meal. Timing is a critical factor. I usually make a time line showing all the key events so that I don't forget anything.

The following time line illustrates the organization necessary for serving everything at the appropriate moment. The menu is baked rice, fried tofu, aduki beans, gravy, sautéed vegetables, seaweed, and bancha-twig tea. The first thing to do is to make a complete list of everything to be served at the meal. Post both list and time line in plain sight of all cooks and helpers.

Evening Meal - 100 people

6:30 p.m.

Baked Brown Rice

Stir-Fry Vegetables Yeast Gravy

Arame Seaweed Aduki Beans
Bancha-Twig Tea
(NO SILVERWARE - CHOPSTICKS only:)

8:00 AM - SOAK BEANS
4:30 PM START COOKING BEANS
         START BAKING RICE
4:45   START COOKING SEAWEED
5:00   CHOP VEGETABLES
5:15   START TEA
5:20   MAKE GRAVY
5:30   START FRYING TOFU
5:45   START SAUTEING VEGGIES
6:00   BEGIN SERVING
6:25

Cost effectiveness

SIX POUNDS OF STEEL-CUT OATMEAL cost less than three dollars and provide one hundred and twenty people with their main breakfast dish. That's less than three cents per serving. One fifty-cent cup of miso paste added to leftover beans, vegetables, gravy, and water can make a nutritious soup for a hundred lunches. Since soy products, such as tempeh and tofu, cost about half the price per pound as red meat, there is much to be saved by using them. As I write, wheat berries cost twenty-two cents per pound. Whole-wheat bread made on the premises with freshly ground flour is probably the most cost-effective food of all.

Some natural foods seem expensive when compared to their processed, denatured counterparts. However, these foods not only stretch further for the cook, but also further at the table — diners are satisfied by smaller servings. A good example would be white-flour spaghetti versus buckwheat soba noodles. White pasta costs a dollar per pound while the soba costs a dollar seventy-five.

But it takes close to three pounds of white pasta to feed every fifteen people, while it only takes half as much soba. The amazing thing is that, in addition to being cost-effective, natural whole grains, beans, and their products are absolutely the highest-quality foods you can buy at any price. Whole natural foods also help one eliminate expensive red meat and costly, overprocessed, adulterated packaged foods while providing an alternative superior both in nutrition and taste.

Hot and cold cereals made from whole grains such as oats, wheat, barley, or rice are far superior and less costly than the sugar-laced, shot-from-guns versions that come in brightly colored boxes. When you buy a processed cereal, you are paying not only for the cereal, but also for sweeteners, boxes designed by artists and psychologists, and a lot of advertising. All you really need is the cereal: fifty pounds of high-quality rolled oats from a natural-food supplier costs about fifteen dollars. Fifty pounds of packaged, processed cereal costs over ninety dollars.

Cost comparison of natural foods vs. factory-processed foods

One pound of high-quality whole-wheat bread will cost $1.00 to $1.75 per pound. You can make it in your own kitchen for twenty-five cents per pound. A group of one hundred fifty people eat thirty pounds of bread a day. In a seven-month season we save $7,000 just on bread!

Freshly made pasta costs six cents a serving. The factory version will cost twenty cents a serving.

Factory salad dressings made with low-quality ingredients will cost more than if you make it yourself using the finest ingredients, including pure olive oil!

Equal-quality pancake mixes will cost twenty-five cents a pound by making it yourself versus $1.25 a pound — that is a five-hundred-percent difference!

Tempeh costs $2.00 a pound less than meat. Each pound feeds the same number of people without the nutritional problems of meat!

Coffee costs are less per serving with freshly ground beans than with packaged products, plus the coffee taste from freshly ground beans is noticeably superior.

Managing leftovers

A COOK MAY OFTEN WANT to plan a meal based on a specific leftover food such as cooked grain. First of all, you have to have an idea of how much food is likely to be consumed at any particular meal. Estimating this correctly comes from experience with your group. The quantities given in this book are for Outward Bound students who are active and very hungry — so if you are cooking for a retirement home, expect leftovers! The key is to plan meals that allow for creative use of leftovers in the next day's menu. For example, extra baked or sautéed vegetables combined with cooked grains can make quick, easy, low-cost, yet nutritious soups and stews. If you take the leftovers from an evening meal of rice, vegetables, beans, seaweed, and gravy, you will have the makings of a wonderful soup and need only add water. Season with tamari or miso — just heat and serve.

Leftover morning cereals should go into unleavened bread. Evening grains can be added to bread dough or soups, stir-fried, or made into grain salads. Leftover beans can be refried for lunch protein or put into soups and stews. Unused bread should be cubed and dried for croutons, bread puddings, and plain old bread crumbs. Herbal teas can be chilled overnight and served as delightful iced teas at lunch the next day — or mixed with fruit juice for punch.

Leftover rules

1. If it is over three days old, compost it.

2. If you are not sure it's still good, assume it isn't!

3. If it doesn't get eaten the second time around, it never will.

4. Dressed salads never last through the night.

5. Nothing can ever be made from a leftover casserole!

Taste

AS I EAT THIS PIECE of unleavened oat-meal bread — I am tasting. Just what goes into the event called tasting? I do not taste merely bread, I taste *great* bread! What makes it so great?

The food

Freshness — Made from freshly ground whole-wheat flours and grains.

Method — Prepared with an "appropriate" method.

Quality — Freshest, highest-quality food — no chemicals, colorings, preservatives in either the bread itself or in the ingredients that went into it.

The cook

Knowledge — The cook that made it knew how to properly prepare the dough as well as cook it for the right amount of time.

Proper attitude — The cook had a positive attitude toward the food, toward his or her position in the kitchen as well as life in general.

The eater

My own *habits, likes, and dislikes,* coupled with my *cultural background,* my *eating history,* the *environment* at that moment, my particular *attitude* today along with my *expectations* of what I thought it was going to taste like . . . make it a tasty food to me at this moment.

Consider all of these as you cook . . . and you will succeed in serving tasty food!

3. Real foods

Whole grains

Wheat

The whole-wheat berry or kernel that we know today arrived on the scene at the dawn of civilization. It brought about the shift from hunting and gathering to agrarian communities. From wheat comes bread, the staff of life. Good bread can be the cornerstone of a diet.

Wheat is available in several varieties and forms. Whole-wheat berries can be ground into flour or meal, or cracked. Bulgur is precooked cracked wheat that is quickly prepared. Pastry wheat, best suited to pie and cake recipes, is sweeter, and has larger, whiter, and starchier kernels. Whole-wheat pastry flour contains little or no gluten so that cookies and crusts come out light and flaky. By contrast, Durham wheat is high in gluten and is a very dense and yellow grain. It is most often used to make pasta. Hard red winter wheat makes the best bread flour, although some people prefer slightly cakier breads made from gold and silver varieties.

Rye

Rye is a strongly flavored grain traditionally associated with a rigorous peasant existence. Rye flakes can be added to bread dough, hot cereals, and baked grain dishes. When adding rye flour to bread dough, remember that it contains little or no gluten, so your bread will not rise as high as usual.

Buckwheat

Kasha — hulled, roasted, and cracked buckwheat — is becoming familiar to Americans. Raw buckwheat groats are also available, but I have found little use for them. Because buckwheat has a very strong flavor which most Americans are unfamiliar with, I recommend serving it in combination with milder-tasting grains. Buckwheat adds strength to hot cereals, muffins, and pancakes on cold winter mornings.

Corn

Corn, the sweetest of all grains, is a traditional American staple. But the de-germed, devitalized version of cornmeal sold in our supermarkets today is far from what the native Americans gave to the Pilgrims! Dried corn, essential to any grain room, will yield cornmeal, grits, and corn flour. A stone mill will release its full taste and nutritional value. You will be amazed at the hearty flavor of your cornbreads and muffins if you use freshly ground grains. In season, fresh corn on the cob can be baked, boiled, or steamed. A very prominent grain in South American cuisine, corn is a great vehicle to take your group south of the border.

Oats

Horses love oats, and for a good reason. Oats are well known for their ability to provide stamina. For centuries, the Scotch have cooked them for breakfast to counteract the Highland chill. Oats are a relatively sweet grain, which makes them especially suitable for breakfast. There is a vast qualitative difference between store-bought, boxed rolled oats and the rolled oats available in bulk from a natural-foods wholesaler. I keep three forms of oats on hand: whole oats for flour and Irish oatmeal, rolled oats for cereals and breads, and steel-cut oats for a hearty breakfast cereal.

Millet

Millet is an underused grain, delicious if prepared correctly, and loaded with nutrition. Baked millet can be served in place of potatoes, and the average person will find it a pleasant change. It is a good grain to introduce early in the transition diet. (See specific recipes.)

Quinoa

Quinoa (pronounced keen-wa) is now available through most natural-food wholesalers. It is high in protein and trace minerals. It was once the staple food of the Incas. It cooks up quickly, in about twenty minutes, and has a unique nut-like flavor. It is well worth trying.

Brown Rice

Rice is the primary staple for about half of the world's population. There is a good reason for its popularity. Brown rice contains complex carbohydrates, proteins, fats, minerals, and vitamins all in proportions excellent for human consumption. Most B vitamins are destroyed when brown rice is milled into white rice, and the important ratio of nutrients inherent in all whole foods is also destroyed.

There are four types of brown rice available in this country today: short-, medium-, long-grain, and sweet. Short-grain is the heartiest variety, ideal for colder climates, while medium- and long-grain rice make fluffier, lighter dishes. Sweet brown rice is a good grain for summer and is perfect for dessert recipes.

Flour

Not every brand of whole-wheat flour is as good as its label claims. The best whole-wheat flour is stone ground just before you buy it — or, ideally, ground in your own kitchen. Most natural-food stores either have their own stone mill or purchase stone-ground flour from a natural-food wholesaler. It is best to buy flour as you need it. If you must store it for more than a few days, refrigerate.

As soon as the wheat kernels are broken open during the grinding process, nutrients and flavor begin to disappear through oxidation. White flour has been devitalized to such an extent that there is nothing left that will oxidize, so it can be stored indefinitely — a solution to storage problems, but it is such an impoverished food that there is no point in storing it at all.

The amazing soybean

THE VERSATILE SOYBEAN is truly the food of the future. As population increases and it is no longer feasible to raise so much animal protein, mankind will be forced to rely more on the complete protein available from soybeans. A well-integrated menu should include a wide variety of soy products — miso, tamari, tempeh, tofu, soy milk, and, of course, plain soybeans.

Soybeans are the only vegetable source that contains complete protein. (Soy contains all of the eight essential amino acids that are needed to build cells.) In addition, soybean protein complements the partial proteins in many other foods, boosting their nutritional value.

Miso

Miso, a thick paste that varies from beige to dark brown in color, is made by fermenting soybeans, salt, and, frequently, grains for long periods under specific conditions. It is an excellent base for soups. I think of it as a meat-flavored soup base without meat. There are many varieties and flavors of miso: hatcho has the strongest, saltiest flavor, while mugi and genmai are slightly milder, and mellow white miso is quite sweet. Try them all to get a feeling for their tastes.

Tamari

Tamari, the real soy sauce, is another fermented soybean product. It is a far cry from the caramelized, salted water and molasses that passes for commercial soy sauce. Tamari can replace salt in most grain-based meals and soups, and is an essential seasoning in many of my recipes. You can purchase tamari in bulk quantities, so it need not be expensive. I always keep a pitcher of tamari handy while cooking. For a simple broth in which to serve soba noodles, mix one part tamari with eight parts hot water.

Tempeh

Tempeh is a cultured soy product made from whole soybeans. Soybeans are very difficult to digest unless some drastic cooking or fermentation process has transformed them. Thus the Orientals ferment them to make tamari and miso; mash and curdle them to make tofu; and introduce a friendly bacteria that predigests them to make tempeh. Usually sold in eight-ounce packages, the several varieties available come plain or mixed with grains. Tempeh is tastiest baked or fried. Prepared and served properly, tempeh often becomes a new favorite thanks to its "fried chicken" taste.

Tofu

If tempeh tastes like chicken, then tofu could be likened to a delicate white fish. Tofu's strength is its ability to blend with other flavors without conflict. It has little or no taste of its own, so it goes well in many different settings.

Legumes

LEGUMES, SUCH AS BLACK BEANS and chickpeas, are high-quality protein. This is an important part of the transition diet since it is the chief protein complement to the grains you will be serving. The effect of eating grains and legumes at the same meal or at least in the same day is that the partial proteins of each combine to make complete proteins. Legumes are also an excellent source of fiber and carbohydrate. However, inadequately cooked legumes cause real digestive problems. Make sure that you cook them long enough — they should be very tender. Each variety has its own distinct character.

Oil

VEGETABLE OIL IS MADE by roasting, crushing, and pressing the seeds and fruits of various flowering plants. Most vegetable-oil companies use extreme temperatures and pressure to obtain high oil yields. Unfortunately, this process lessens the nutritional content considerably. Worse yet, chemical solvents are used to extract an even higher percentage of oil. Not only does this cause further nutritional loss, but it also adds the residual chemicals to your dinner menu. To top it off, chemical preservatives and so-called enhancing agents (bleaches, deodorants, anticoagulants, and so on) are added to extend the shelf life and add to the visual appeal of these inferior products. It is in your best interest to avoid these refined, adulterated oils.

Natural-food suppliers and co-ops carry unrefined or cold-pressed oils. Neither preserved, chemically adulterated, nor filtered to the extent that commercial oils are, they have not been heated to extreme temperatures. These oils have the flavor of the food from which they are pressed and great nutritional value. Athough the cost of unrefined or cold-pressed oils runs about forty percent higher than their commercial counterparts, unrefined oil will go about twice as far in use.

Note: It is wise to refrigerate all natural oils in warm weather.

Safflower oil – Safflower oil is the most popular and usually the most inexpensive natural oil. It is a great all-purpose product and is high in polyunsaturated fat as well as in linoleic acids.

Sunflower oil – Sunflower oil is another all-purpose oil. It has a slightly stronger flavor than safflower oil, but keeps better in hot weather.

Corn oil – Corn oil is good for breads and general baking purposes. It foams up when heated, so it is not good for frying, and its thick texture and strong flavor make it less suitable for salads. It is loaded with vitamin E, so it keeps well. Vitamin E acts as an antioxidant in the oil as well as in your body.

Soy oil – Soy oil is another very heavy oil, great for general baking and loaded with nutritional value.

Sesame oil – Sesame oil is a mild, light oil with a tasty, nutty flavor. It is good for almost everything and is especially suitable for salads. Unfortunately, it is very expensive.

Olive oil – Olive oil is the king of oils. It makes a delicious sauté and is the best salad oil available. Extra-virgin olive oil is not inexpensive, but is well worth the money.

Peanut oil – Peanut oil is a good all-purpose oil ideal for frying because of its stability. If you like peanuts, you will love unrefined peanut oil. It is very reasonably priced.

Sweeteners

THERE ARE GOOD REASONS to cut down on one's sugar intake. Sugar (pure white) is devoid of vitamins, minerals, and fiber. It contains what nutritionists call empty calories. Since the nutrients have been refined out of it, the body must deplete its own supply in order to metabolize the sugar. And it is quite clear that excessive sugar intake causes dental cavities.

Part of my transitional approach is to substitute the more beneficial sweeteners for sugar before cutting down on it. Use unrefined honey, molasses, sorghum, real maple syrup, and barley malt, which do contain vitamins and minerals. Don't bother with overpriced "raw" sugar. It is only a shade less refined than white sugar and is in no way significantly more healthful. It is what I would call a "token" natural food.

Red meat

RED MEAT IS EXPENSIVE, hard to digest, and loaded with saturated fats. In addition, the meat available in today's supermarkets comes from animals raised on chemical diets and injected with drugs to speed growth and increase tenderness. More and more researchers are confirming the need for Americans to cut down on meat consumption.

With a diet based on whole grains naturally high in fiber, there is a rapid, efficient transit of food through the intestines. By contrast, a diet based on refined white flour, sugar, and the excessive consumption of meat results in much slower transit times. It is fat in meat that slows the digestion. A slow digestion means toxins stay in the gastrointestinal tract longer, allowing more time for absorption before they are excreted.

Seaweeds

I PREFER TO CALL THEM sea vegetables because "weeds" would suggest to the average person that they are a last-resort food. You should give the people you cook for some preparation before serving sea vegetables, or you may find them all coming back uneaten. (Why are seaweeds such a problem? Fear? Visions of sea monsters frolicking about in slimy weeds?) It is really too bad that so many people are reluctant to try them because they can be quite delicious. What is more, seaweeds are rich in trace minerals, especially iodine, copper, calcium, as well as the B vitamins. They are twenty to thirty percent protein and provide a terrific source of many nutrients often virtually absent from the American diet. I have found the most useful seaweeds readily available to be hijiki, arame, nori, and wakame. Most natural-food stores carry these plus a few other varieties.

Yogurt

YOGURT IS A DAIRY PRODUCT made by adding one of several specific varieties of bacteria to milk that alter its flavor, texture, and digestibility. These are referred to as "friendly" bacteria because they actually promote a healthy strain of digestive bacteria in our intestines, which in turn helps us to assimilate more fully the nutrients in our food. For some people who have difficulty digesting dairy products, yogurt causes the fewest problems. However, if you load it with sugar, its nutritional value is diminished. Yogurt can be served plain or with natural sweeteners or fruit.

Spices

IT IS VERY CONVENIENT to purchase ground spices and herbs in neat little containers from the local supermarket. However, the taste and quality of what you serve will be far below the level that is within your reach with just a little effort.

Commercial iodized salt is treated with chemical whiteners and anticlogging agents that may be detrimental to health. It is far better to use unrefined sea salt which contains hard-to-find trace minerals but no unnecessary chemicals. Sea salt does not contain iodine, but if other seafoods are present in the diet iodine intake should be adequate. Sea salt tastes a touch stronger than commercial salt, so use a little less. Lately, excessive salt has been seen as an aggravator of high blood pressure, so don't overdo it.

There is a world of difference between factory-ground black pepper and peppercorns freshly ground in your own kitchen. Pepper grinders are very easy to find. Buy whole black peppercorns and grind as needed. At Hurricane Island I use a small electric spice mill to grind many fresh spices. Other spices that can be bought as seeds and ground fresh are coriander, cumin, mustard, anise, and fennel. Take the time. The flavor and quality of freshly ground spices can make the difference between a merely good dish and a truly superior one.

Beverages

THE QUALITY OF WATER is very important both for drinking and cooking. If the water in your kitchen is not clear and tasty, look into getting a filtration system.

Commercial soft drinks (primarily sugar and water) are very bad news nutritionally, and the low-calorie ones (artificial sweeteners and water) are just as bad. It is amazing how many soft drinks are consumed every year in this country. They are a major source of the average American's excessive sugar intake. Apparently, the latest artificial sweeteners actually create a bigger craving for sweets because their sweet taste cheats the digestive system. It prepares to metabolize sugar, but there is none there.

Fruit juices or fruit juice concentrates are available from most natural-food wholesalers. Combine these with herb teas or sparkling water to make drinks infinitely superior to anything on the institutional market.

Common black tea — the sort sold in boxes of a hundred tea bags — is not usually a high-quality product. Most institutional teas contain dyes to make them look stronger than they actually are. It is far better to purchase bulk teas. Add three or four handfuls to one forty-quart pot of hot water that has been boiled, to make enough tea for a hundred and fifty people. Let steep from three to seven minutes, then strain and serve.

Considering the problems often caused by black tea — nervousness, acid stomach, caffeine addiction — I prefer to offer nonstimulating herbal teas, particularly with the evening meal. But remember that many so-called herbal teas contain maté, a stimulating tea high in caffeine. (Brazilian natives drink maté all day long to combat the hot climate.) There are many nonstimulating herbal teas available today which can replace black tea quite successfully.

Make extra herb tea for the evening meal so that you can serve it iced with lunch the next day, or mixed with fruit juice as a punch. My favorite tea with grain-based evening meals is bancha- (or kukicha) twig tea. It refreshes the palate.

If your diners insist on coffee, give them real coffee. Fresh whole-bean coffee costs half as much as packaged commercial brands if you take into account the yield per pound. Store large quantities of whole-bean coffee in the freezer until needed.

However, there are good reasons not to drink coffee — jangled nerves, caffeine addiction. So I serve coffee only once a day at breakfast. At lunch I offer fruit juice or punch, and at dinner an herb tea.

Chemically decaffeinated coffee is processed with such harsh chemicals that I would not use it at all. "Water-processed" decaffeinated coffee, however, is quite delicious and evidently poses less of a health risk. There are also many grain-based and nut-based coffee substitutes.

Chocolate drinks can be successfully replaced with carob drinks. Chocolate has lots of sugar and has caffeine. Carob is naturally sweeter than chocolate.

4. Kitchen equipment

KEEP IN MIND THAT no amount of equipment will make up for a poor attitude or an improper approach toward food. Many cooks will be in a kitchen that already provides most of the equipment needed for whole foods, with the exception of a flour mill. Many large kitchens also have such tools as power mixers, only used for mixing instant foods, or ovens only used to warm frozen, portion-controlled patties.

Except for a stove, counters, and a sink, everything else is optional. The equipment you need will be determined by the number of people you must serve, your budget, and the space available.

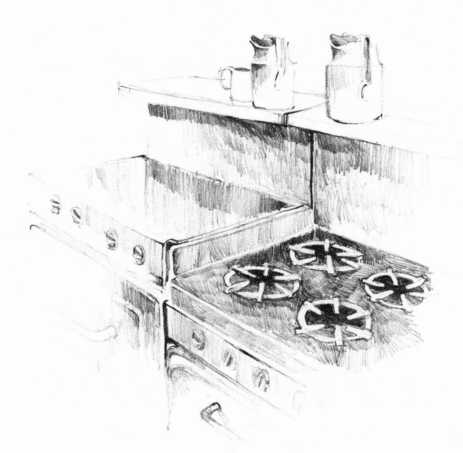

Commercial stove

I recommend a range with six burners, two ovens, and a grill and prefer a gas range to an electric. A stove of this size is adequate for cooks serving fifteen to seventy-five people, and if you add a pizza oven, the numbers are substantially increased. If you anticipate doing a lot of baking, an extra oven or two will prove useful. Most restaurant suppliers carrying a full line of commercial stoves sell them at prices ranging from $1,800 to $4,000. Used stoves run fifty to sixty percent less. The Hurricane Island kitchen has two ranges as described above, and one two-bay pizza oven. These three units are adequate for serving an average of a hundred people three meals a day as well as supplying breads for a hundred more.

Flour mill

A flour mill does not just make bread flour. Rather, it opens to you and the people you serve a whole new world of nutrition and variety. Freshly ground whole-wheat pastry flour, cornmeal, buckwheat flour, millet flour, rice cream, freshly cracked oatmeal and rye meal will naturally take their place and in your menus. You will be amazed at how often you will want to use your mill and will wonder how you ever got along without it.

I have used Meadows* eight-inch stone mills for over fifteen years. I have one mill that is over twelve years old and is still going strong. I suggest purchasing a mill for any kitchen regularly serving fifteen people or more. In my experience, it is the most essential piece of equipment after a stove and a sink. The savings for a community of fifty will pay for a mill in only ten months, if you grind twenty pounds of grain per day at a cost that is ten cents lower per pound than the equivalent factory-ground products. I feel very strongly about the value of this type of mill when integrating natural foods into a large-group setting.

*Meadows Mill Co., P.O. Box 1288, North Wilkesboro, NC 28659.

Steam table

A steam table is certainly convenient if you regularly serve large groups. For greatest success, minimize the time that the food sits in it. A steam table is great for warming up soups and chowders without scorching them, although double boilers can perform the same task without the high cost.

Power mixer

Made by various companies, power mixers come in a wide range of sizes, with many attachments available. My basic bread recipes are designed to fit well in a thirty-quart mixer bowl. A twenty-quart mixer is fine for up to seventy-five people. It costs about $2,500. The attachments most often used are the mixing paddle, bread hook, and wire whisk. I also find a pastry-cutting hook useful for large quantities of pie crust.

Blender

To my mind blenders are overrated. I resort to a blender only when absolutely necessary. If there is a reasonably convenient way to do something by hand, I prefer it. However, a blender does have its place if used with discretion. Home-sized blenders cannot stand up to commercial use for very long. I recommend using a stainless-steel "bar blender." A one-quart unit costs about $125, while a one-gallon blender costs close to $1,000.

Slicer

Slicers are usually used for foods you will no longer be serving such as luncheon meats. Nevertheless, you will find one useful for slicing unleavened bread and cheese.

Refrigeration

Adequate refrigeration space is a must. With a little carpentry and a lot of work, you can make your own cooler box for about a tenth the cost of having a commercial one installed. Have a local carpenter frame up the size box that you need, line it with triple insulation, and then have a refrigeration company install the cooling unit.

Freezer

Freezers allow you to stock up on breads and other basic items. They can also be used to store vegetables for unanticipated meals. If proper freezing techniques are used, you can offer emergency vegetable dishes at short notice with no significant drop in quality.

Spice mill

A spice mill costs very little, but is essential. It will enhance your cooking more than any other piece of equipment. Herbs and spices lose flavor once they are ground, as do grains. A mortar and pestle or a Japanese suribachi will do the job, although I recommend purchasing a small electric coffee grinder to be used, but not for coffee, for spices. We use one for herbs and spices such as peppercorns, anise, coriander, mustard seed, or fennel — grinding them as needed.

Fryolator

Deep-fried foods have been associated with heart disease and indigestion for many years. However, fryolators are not to blame, but rather the saturated fats most commonly used. If you decide to use a fryolator, use vegetable oil in it rather than solid shortening.

Cutlery

As you slant toward vegetarian cooking, you will find that Japanese cutlery may meet your needs better than common knives. At home I prefer to use high-carbon steel knives, for they can be given the sharpest edge. However, in a situation where students and staff are helping in the kitchen I find that stainless-steel knives hold their edge longer. The cutting edge of a knife tells you a great deal about the food being served and the cooks involved.

5. Ordering staples and setting up a grain room

DEPENDING ON THE size of your operation, you can use a corner of your kitchen or devote an entire room to grains, beans, and a flour mill. In any event, I suggest you purchase rubber or plastic containers with airtight lids for the many varieties of grains and beans that you will want to store. Rubbermaid makes a complete line of barrels called "Brute" that come in ten- to fifty-gallon sizes. I have used them for years and found them to be virtually indestructible. They come in many colors. You may want to order them in "food-service white."

I store basic foods in the following quantities. This list may be especially helpful if you are stocking your kitchen with whole foods for the first time. If you do not have a flour mill, then remember to order flour and meal instead of whole-grain berries and kernels. In addition to the barrels, I store unopened fifty-pound bags of the items most frequently used, stacking them neatly on pallets. This is for a kitchen that serves an average of a hundred people a day.

Item	Quantity in pounds	Barrel size in gallons
Aduki beans (azuki)	25	12
Barley	50	12
Brown rice, shortgrain	50-100	20
Brown rice, sweet	50	12
Buckwheat kasha	50	12
Bulgur	50-100	20
Chickpeas (garbanzos)	25	12
Corn, whole	50-100	20

Item	Quantity in pounds	Barrel size in gallons
Kidney beans	25	12
Lentils, green	25	12
Millet	50	12
Oats, rolled	50-100	30
Oats, steel-cut	50	20
Oats, whole	50	12
Peanuts, shelled	25	12
Pinto beans	25	12
Popcorn	25	12
Rye berries	50	12
Rye flakes	25	12
Sesame seeds	50	20
Soybeans	50	12
Split peas, green	25	12
Sunflower seeds	25	12
Wheat berries, hard	100-150	30
Wheat berries, soft	100-150	30
Wheat flakes	25	12

I keep the following basics on hand:

Arrowroot starch	5	pounds	Molasses	5	gallons
Barley malt	5	gallons	Nutritional yeast*	20	pounds
Brown sugar	50	pounds	Olive oil*	1	gallon
Carob powder	20	pounds	Peanut oil*	5	gallons
Cashew pieces	25	pounds	Powdered milk	50	pounds
Cider vinegar	5	gallons	Red wine vinegar	5	gallons
Coconut, shredded	25	pounds	Safflower oil*	5	gallons
Date pieces*	30	pounds	Sea salt	50	pounds
Dried apples*	25	pounds	Sesame tahini*	5	gallons
Honey	60	pounds	Tamari soy sauce	5	gallons
Maple syrup*	2	gallons	Toasted sesame oil	1	quart
Miso paste	40	pounds	Walnut pieces*	25	pounds

* These items should be refrigerated, if possible, as should all flours and meals.

PART II
The recipes: preparing basic whole foods

1. Whole-grain recipes

Baked Grains

This is the most important page in the book. Use it!
Yield – 45 servings per 12- x 20- x 4-inch "hotel tray."
Quantities are given per tray.

Grain	Amount (cups)	Liquid (cups)	Cooking time (hours)
Brown rice, short-grain	14	26	1½
Brown rice, long-grain	14	24	1½
Brown rice, sweet	14	28	1½
Barley	11	26	2
Millet	10	26	2
Bulgur	16	24	1
Kasha	16	24	1

First, lightly sauté half a pound of diced onions — and an equal amount of chopped mushrooms if desired — in an oiled tray. Use about three-quarters of a cup of oil per tray. Cook till just tender, then add the grain of your choice and continue sautéing for about five minutes over a medium flame. When the grain is well coated with oil and lightly sautéed, add the hot water or broth and bring to a low boil. Then cover with foil and place in a preheated 350°F oven and bake for the time indicated.

Combination Grains – Baked

Combination – grain dishes also work well. The following combinations all fit in a standard hotel tray. Both the procedure and yield are identical to those in the preceding recipe.

Grains	Plus...	Liquid (cups)	Cooking Time (hours)
10 cups rice	4 cups wheat flakes	24	1½
10 cups rice	4 cups sesame seeds	24	1½
10 cups bulgur	6 cups kasha	24	1½
8 cups millet	4 cups kasha	24	1½

In general, a third of a cup of dry grain yields one serving cooked. As you can see, the quantity of water required to cook specific grains varies only slightly.

As a rule, I prefer baking grains rather than boiling them. It gets them off of the stove top and out of the way, and is an almost foolproof method of cooking grains.

Cooking Brown Rice

An eight-quart pot will hold ten cups of rice in twenty cups of water, and will make thirty servings. Bring to a boil, cover, and simmer for about one hour. If you are feeding sixty people, simply use two pots.

Pressure-Cooking Brown Rice

Some people feel that pressure-cooking brown rice is the best method. Pressure-cooked rice is denser and chewier. Start with one and a half cups of water to one cup of rice. Place water and rice in a pressure cooker, seal the lid, and bring up to fifteen pounds pressure. Cook for about twenty minutes. The various types of rice differ slightly in their cooking requirements. Short-grain brown rice absorbs more water than medium- and long-grain.

Breakfast Foods

Rice Cream

Yield – 45 servings

Rice cream is a wonderful alternative to breakfast oatmeal. It is delicious served with traditional hot cereal toppings. It is usually made from sweet brown rice that has been dry-toasted, then ground in a mill or blender to a coarse meal. I recommend toasting it on cookie sheets till golden brown, then running it through your flour mill at a very coarse setting.

8 cups toasted, ground sweet brown rice
36 cups boiling water
1-2 tablespoons sea salt

Stir the ground rice into the salted boiling water. Stir with a whisk to avoid lumps. Cover and simmer over a low heat for one hour, or simmer in a double boiler over a very low flame overnight.

Cream Cereals - Mixed Grains

As with baked grain combinations, there are many delicious grain mixes that can come under the heading of breakfast cream cereals. Toast and grind the grain as described above. The flour portion of any freshly ground cereal rises to the top and prevents the water from reaching the bulk of the grain. Be sure to stir the cereal thoroughly before turning down the heat and leaving it overnight. The following combinations work well. However, there are virtually infinite possibilities!

Sweet Rice and Kasha

Servings	15	30	60	90	120	
Rice	2	4	8	12	16	cups
Kasha	1	2	4	6	8	cups
Water	12	24	48	72	96	cups
Salt	½	1	2	3	4	tablespoons

Rice - Millet - Kasha

Servings	15	30	60	90	120	
Rice	1	2	4	6	8	cups
Millet	1	2	4	6	8	cups
Kasha	1	2	4	6	8	cups
Water	12	24	48	72	96	cups
Salt	½	1	2	3	4	tablespoons

Follow the instructions for *Rice Cream* on the previous page.

Freshly Ground Oatmeal (Irish Oatmeal)

Set your flour mill for a very coarse grind, just enough to crack whole oat groats in two. The resulting oatmeal will be a combination of oat pieces and flour — herein lies the secret to its creaminess. This oatmeal takes a good thirty minutes to cook, so watch it carefully. To avoid burning the bottom, stir often over a low heat. Using a double boiler overnight works well, as with steel-cut oatmeal. However, because of its flour content, this cereal tends to settle on the bottom of the pot and will stay there all night unless you make sure it is thoroughly suspended before leaving it. For a darker, richer flavor, try roasting the oats before milling. To roast, spread the groats on cookie sheets and bake for twenty minutes at 375°F or till light brown in color.

Irish Oatmeal - Basic

Servings	15	30	60	90	120	
Water	11	22	44	66	88	cups
Oats, cracked	4	8	16	24	32	cups
Salt	1	2	3	4	5	tablespoons

Morning Cereal

Servings	15	30	60	90	120	
Water	12	24	48	72	96	cups
Butter	¼	½	1	1½	2	pounds
Salt	½	1	2	3	4	tablespoons
Kasha	2	4	8	12	16	cups
Bulgur	1½	3	6	9	12	cups
Rolled oats	1	2	4	6	8	cups
Powdered milk	1	2	4	6	8	cups
Raisins	1	2	4	6	8	cups
Maple syrup	¼	½	1	1½	2	cups

Bring water to boil, add the rest of the ingredients, and simmer for thirty-five minutes.

Creamy Oatmeal

Yield – 30 servings

24 cups boiling water
1½ tablespoons salt
10 cups rolled oats
2 cups instant milk powder
2 cups sunflower seeds
2 cups raisins
3 apples, cored and chopped

Combine water and salt in an eight-quart pot. Stir in remaining ingredients. Simmer for about thirty minutes.

Hearty Oat Cereal

Yield – 30 servings

24 cups boiling water
2 cups sliced almonds
2 cups wheat flakes
2 cups rye flakes
1 cup raisins
1 tablespoon salt
10 cups rolled oats

Combine all ingredients except oats in an eight-quart pot. Cook till flakes are soft, about fifteen minutes, then add oats and simmer for another twenty to thirty minutes.

Scotch Oatmeal

Steel-cut oats are groats that have been chopped with steel blades. They take a good hour and a half to cook, so I recommend using a double boiler on a low flame overnight.

Servings	15	30	60	90	120	
Water	12	24	48	72	96	cups
Steel-cut oats	4	8	16	24	32	cups
Salt	1	2	3	4	5	tablespoons

Find the appropriate double boiler(s) with the capacity for your needs. One twenty-four-quart unit is suitable for preparing sixty servings. Set up the double boiler(s), stir the oats into salted water, and cook, covered, on a very low flame overnight. In the morning, turn up the heat for about twenty minutes before serving.

Basic Rolled Oats

Servings	15	30	60	90	120	
Rolled oats	5	10	20	30	40	cups
Water	12	24	48	72	96	cups
Salt	½	1	2	3	4	tablespoons

I recommend using one or more eight-quart pots. Each pot will hold thirty servings. Bring the salted water to a boil, stir in the oats, and simmer for about thirty minutes.

Familia

Yield – 50 servings

Familia or muesli is a popular European breakfast. Serve with yogurt or milk and fresh fruit. Or soak it overnight as they do in Europe in lemon juice and water. It is best to use thin-cut rolled oats because they are to be eaten raw.

30 cups rolled oats
3 cups raisins
3 cups sliced almonds
2 cups brown sugar (optional)
2 cups dried apples, chopped fine
1½ cups coconut, flaked or shredded
1½ cups wheat germ

Combine all ingredients thoroughly. This basic recipe can be varied by substituting other dried fruits and nuts.

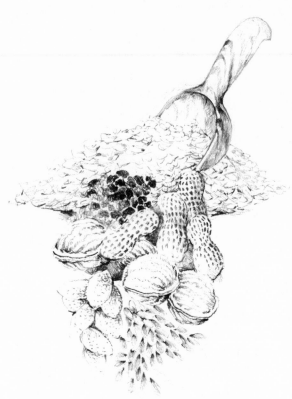

Granola

Yield – 75 servings

I have tried literally dozens of granola recipes, and this is absolutely the best.

4 pounds peanut butter
2½ cups oil
3 cups honey
30 cups rolled oats
6 cups coconut
5 cups rye flakes
10 cups sunflower seeds
4 cups chopped walnuts
4 cups sliced almonds
4 cups rice flakes
4 cups powdered milk
4 cups wheat germ
2 cups whole-wheat pastry flour
3 cups sesame seeds
2 cups soy flour
4 cups hot water
6 cups raisins

In an eight-quart saucepan, melt the first three ingredients. In a separate bowl, mix the dry ingredients well. Stir in the melted peanut butter mixture. Sprinkle in the water. Mix again, then spread evenly on oiled cookie sheets. Bake in a slow 325°F oven for about an hour, stirring occasionally. When cool, add raisins.

Cornmeal Mush

Servings	15	30	60	90	120	
Trays	1	2	4	6	8	
Cornmeal	3	6	12	18	24	cups
Boiling water	6	12	24	36	48	cups
Salt	1	2	4	6	9	tablespoons

Whisk the cornmeal into the boiling water, reduce heat, and simmer for thirty minutes, stirring often. A double boiler may be used to prevent scorching. Pour the cooked cornmeal into well-buttered 11- x 14- x 2-inch trays and chill overnight. The next morning, cut each trayful into fifteen squares and fry on a buttered grill until golden brown. Serve with maple syrup or other sweetener. This is a great side dish.

Home-Fried Potatoes

Considering the popularity of home fries, I am always amazed how few people actually know how to cook them properly. It's always disappointing to be served the freeze-dried, shredded version. Potatoes tend to crowd whole grains out of one's menu, but it's all right to include this breakfast favorite in a balanced diet. Use real potatoes and cook them with care.

1 pound of potatoes for every 4-5 people
1/4 pound chopped onions
1/8 pound butter or oil
1/2 green pepper, chopped

The night before, wash, scrub, but do not peel the potatoes. Cut lengthwise into quarters. Place in pot, cover with lightly salted water, bring to a boil, and cook till just tender. It is better to have them underdone than overcooked and mushy. Strain, reserving the water for your next batch of bread. Allow to cool, cover, and place them in the cooler overnight.

In the morning, while your grill or heavy frying pan is heating up, slice the potatoes into bite-sized chunks. Sauté chopped onions and green peppers in butter or oil. As soon as these begin to sizzle, add the chunked potatoes and stir-fry till golden brown. Season with salt and freshly ground black pepper and serve with a sprinkle of chopped fresh parsley.

Grain Dishes
for Lunch and Dinner

Polenta

Servings	15	30	60	90	120	
Oil	¾	1½	3	4	6	cups
Cornmeal	2	3½	7	10	14	cups
Boiling water	2	4	8	12	16	quarts
Raw chopped vegetables	2	4	8	12	16	quarts

Optional Ingredients

	15	30	60	90	120	
Cheddar cheese	1	2	4	6	8	cups
Parmesan cheese	½	1	2	3	4	cups
Tomatoes, chopped	2	4	8	12	16	cups
Cumin	1	2	4	6	8	tablespoons
Coriander	½	1	2	3	4	tablespoons
Tamari	¼	½	1	1½	2	cups
Chili powder	1	2	4	6	8	tablespoons

Polenta is basically a cornmeal roux, best when mixed with sautéed vegetables and served with beans. Heat the oil, whisk in the cornmeal, and stir till coated with oil. Add the water slowly, whisking all the time, and cook over a low flame till thick. Meanwhile, sauté mixed chopped vegetables such as red onions, summer squash, green peppers, and mushrooms till tender. Add to the cornmeal roux and simmer in a double boiler for thirty minutes. Season with salt and pepper. Add any of the optional ingredients as desired. Serve with boiled kidney or pinto beans. A green salad would balance the colors perfectly. This makes a low-cost yet nutritious meal.

Baked Orange Millet

Yield – 60 servings

3/4 pound butter
14 cups millet
3 cups chopped dried apricots
1½ tablespoons salt
14 cups boiling water
14 cups orange juice
1/4 cup honey

Melt butter in a 12- x 20- x 4-inch hotel tray, and sauté millet for ten to fifteen minutes. Add remaining ingredients and bring to a boil. Cover and place in a preheated 350°F oven for one and a half hours. This is a perfect summer grain dish to serve with fish or poultry and a salad.

Homemade Pasta

Before making pasta for large groups, I suggest that you try it out on a small scale. When you make pasta for a hundred or so people, you will have to use a machine to mix and knead the dough. Making it by hand for a few people first will give you a feeling for the quality of the end product.

Invented by the Chinese, brought to Italy by Marco Polo, pasta is now one of western civilization's favorite foods. As is true of most foods, the very highest-quality pasta is actually less expensive, as long as you are willing to put a little energy into its preparation. It is really quite easy. I've even made it in an open boat with no more than a flat piece of driftwood and a beer bottle. Most novices can make an edible pasta with their first try.

Believe it or not, all you will need are a few *eggs*, a little *flour*, a *smooth surface* to work on, and a *rolling pin*. If you have a pasta machine that has been hiding up in the attic since your wedding, so much the better — but it is not necessary. As for the time involved, one person can make enough pasta for four people in about twenty minutes.

Handmade Fresh Pasta
Yield – 4 servings

2 large eggs
3/4 cup sifted whole-wheat flour
3/4 cup unbleached white flour
1 teaspoon oil
1 teaspoon water

I use half unbleached white flour and half sifted whole-wheat flour. Semolina flour is even better than white if you can find it. Try Italian grocery stores. Durham wheat makes the best whole-wheat flour for pasta and, in fact, semolina is merely the refined version of Durham whole wheat.

Mix the flours and place them in a pile on the middle of your board. Make a volcano shape out of the flour with a crater large enough to hold the eggs without spilling. Break the eggs into it. A teaspoon each of water and oil may be added for a softer dough, which is easier to roll out. Now beat the eggs gently with a fork and slowly blend the flour into them. Bring in the sides of the crater until the eggs are no longer so sloppy that they will run across the board. You should have a sticky mass with some flour still available. Start kneading the mass and dust with flour every time you turn it — but go slowly with the flour to maintain an even-textured glob. You may need additional flour, but if you add it too fast, your dough could break into several pieces that will never come back together again.

Knead, adding flour as necessary, for about ten minutes until you have a piece of leathery dough the size of a baseball. It should be dry enough not to stick to your fingers, but not so dry that it does not cohere when rolled out or put through a pasta machine.

At this point, tear off about one-fourth of the ball. Roll it out with a rolling pin into long, thin pieces about four inches wide. Or put it through a pasta machine. In either case, check the texture. If sticky, dust with flour. If not, don't. Fold it over on itself and roll out again. If sticky, dust as before. Keep rolling and folding until you have a very thin rectangle, a sixteenth of an inch thick, tough and leathery in texture. It should measure about four by ten inches. Dust with flour and set aside until all the dough has been rolled out and shaped.

Try maintaining an even thickness. It is easier with a pasta machine, but there is something very special about hand-rolled pasta. Note that if you are making lasagna, no further cutting is required. Just cook the whole strips — and make the best lasagna you have ever eaten. You may cut the pasta either into fettucini (half-inch-wide strips) or, if you are using a pasta machine, a finer variety like spaghetti or linguini, using a spaghetti-cutting wheel. If cutting by hand, use a sharp knife and try to keep the strips even.

Fresh pasta is soft and flexible compared to the store-bought, dried version. It doesn't take very long to cook. Bring *six quarts of salted water* to a boil. Gently add the fresh pasta and cook for about six to ten minutes or until tender. The best method is to allow the water to come to a foamy boil after the pasta has been added, then stir a few times and taste. It should be almost ready at that point. The most accurate test is to bite the pasta and look at the resulting cross-section of one strand — if it is not quite done, there will be a white floury center. As soon as that has gone, the pasta is done.

Strain, place in a bowl, and stir with a few tablespoons of oil so it does not stick together. Serve with a vegetable and a salad. Top with a traditional red or oil and garlic sauce.

Fresh Pasta for Crowds

Yield	2	4	6	8	pounds
Eggs	6	12	18	24	
Oil	1	2	3	4	tablespoons
Water	1	2	3	4	tablespoons
Whole-wheat flour	3	6	9	12	cups
White flour	2	5	7	10	cups

Blend the wet ingredients in a mixer. Using the bread hook on medium speed, add flours alternately until the dough balls up. Add more flour and knead until the dough becomes leathery. The dough has to be dry enough to roll out but not so dry that it tears and crumbles. The quantity of flour will vary every time!

When the dough is ready to work, slice off an eight-ounce piece, and put it through the pasta machine until it is sufficiently thin, or you can roll it out by hand. Cut into whatever shapes you want. Always cook pasta in plenty of salted water — five quarts of water to one pound of pasta. Stir it off the bottom when cooking large amounts to avoid "spaghetti logs."

2. Breads and other baked goods

Attention!

All of the flour recipes in this book were developed using freshly ground flours. Fresh whole-wheat flour is equivalent in bulk to a triple-sifted, store-bought flour. In other words, you must either triple-sift or use less than these recipes call for if you are using flour from a store. Try using about fifteen percent less to start with. Most baked goods must be gauged by eye rather than mere measurement. Quantities given are guides, but only the cook in you can make it perfect.

Yeast Breads

When you start making bread on an institutional scale, begin with the most basic recipes. I offer two — a one-hundred-percent whole-wheat recipe, and a fifty-percent whole-wheat version. I'd recommend trying the latter first, working up to the former in due course. It takes a little more practice to make a successful all-whole-wheat bread, but it is well worth the effort.

With few exceptions, my yeast-bread recipes have two stages. This method is effective because it gives the yeast a chance to get a good hold on the wheat, so to speak. Oil and salt tend to inhibit the yeast's progress, so they should not be added until the second stage. You may proof the yeast before adding it to the sponge, as I've suggested in the all-whole-wheat recipe.

These recipes all fit in a thirty-quart mixing bowl. The yield is twenty-four to thirty pounds per batch. I usually make long pullman-type loaves of two and a quarter pounds each, which yield about twenty slices per loaf. There are several critical points to watch when making whole-wheat bread. One of the most important is adding the correct amount of flour during the second stage — incorporate it slowly until the dough is no longer sticky, but not too stiff. The best rule of thumb is that when the dough begins to pull away from the sides of the mixing bowl and is not very sticky to the touch, then it is very close to being ready. Do not let the yeast overproof — too hot a temperature or too much rising time will deplete the yeast's energy. There are many fine books on the market devoted entirely to bread-making. Making bread on a large scale with a power mixer is actually easier than making it at home by hand.

Lecithin Oil Mix

You can make the very best nonstick coating for your bread and muffin tins by mixing one part liquid lecithin with eight to ten parts oil. Liquid lecithin is made by Fearn Natural Foods (P.O. Box 09398, Milwaukee, Wisconsin 53209) and most natural-food wholesalers carry their products.

Basic Bread - 50% Whole-Wheat

Yield – 10 to 12 loaves, 2¼ pounds each

6 tablespoons dry yeast
18 cups lukewarm water
3 cups sweetener
24 cups whole-wheat flour
5 tablespoons salt
2 cups oil
12 cups unbleached white flour
More flour as needed (12 - 36 cups)

Combine the first four ingredients in a mixing bowl to make a sponge. Let it sit in a warm, draft-free place until doubled in bulk — about forty-five minutes. A gas oven with pilot light is a perfect place. Add the remaining ingredients while mixing with a bread hook. It should start to look like . . . bread dough! Keep adding flour until the dough pulls away from the sides of the bowl and is not too sticky. Remove the dough from the mixing bowl and place in a large, oiled pan. Cover with plastic wrap and allow to rise in a pilot-light oven or other warm, draft-free place until doubled in bulk. Then punch down; allow to rise again till doubled; punch down once more. Now form the dough into loaves. Place them in well-oiled bread pans. Let loaves rise in pans for about twenty-five minutes or until they are fifty percent higher. Bake in a pre-heated oven at 350°F for about an hour.

Basic Bread - 100% Whole-Wheat

Yield – 10 to 12 loaves, 2¼ pounds each

4 cups lukewarm water
6 tablespoons dry yeast
3 tablespoons honey or other sweetener
14 cups lukewarm water
3 cups sweetener
24 cups whole-wheat flour
5 tablespoons salt
2 cups oil
More whole-wheat flour as needed (24 - 48 cups)

To proof the yeast, combine the first three ingredients in a mixing bowl.
When the yeast foams, add the next three ingredients to make a sponge.
Let it sit in a warm, draft-free place until bubbles form and it has
doubled in bulk.

Add the remaining ingredients while mixing with a bread hook. Keep adding flour until the dough pulls away from the sides of the bowl and is not too sticky. Remove the dough from the mixing bowl, place in a large pan, cover with plastic wrap, and allow to rise in a pilot-light oven or other warm, draft-free place until doubled in bulk. Then punch down; allow to rise again till doubled; punch down once more. Now form the dough into loaves. Place them in well-oiled pans. Let the loaves rise in pans for about twenty-five minutes or until they are fifty percent higher. Bake in a preheated 350°F oven for about one hour.

Anadama Bread with Corn and Molasses

Yield – 10 to 12 loaves, 2¼ pounds each

3 cups lukewarm water
6 tablespoons dry yeast
3 tablespoons molasses
14 cups lukewarm coffee
3 cups molasses
18 cups whole-wheat flour
8 cups cornmeal
5 tablespoons salt
2 cups oil
10 cups unbleached white flour
More whole-wheat flour as needed (8 - 24 cups)

To proof the yeast, combine the first three ingredients in a mixing bowl. When the yeast foams, add the following four ingredients to make a sponge. Let rise until doubled, then add the remaining ingredients while mixing with a bread hook. Set dough in a large pan and allow to rise in a pilot-light oven or other warm, draft-free place until doubled in bulk. Then punch down; allow to rise again till doubled; punch down once more. Now form the dough into loaves. Place them in well-oiled pans and let rise for about twenty-five minutes or until they are fifty percent higher. Bake in a preheated 350°F oven for about one hour.

Millet Bread

Yield – 10 to 12 loaves, 2¼ pounds each

6 tablespoons dry yeast
17 cups lukewarm water
3 cups honey
3 cups whole millet
24 cups whole-wheat flour
5 tablespoons salt
2 cups oil
12 cups whole-wheat flour
More whole-wheat flour as needed (24 - 36 cups)

To make the sponge, combine the first five ingredients in a mixing bowl and put in a warm, draft-free place. When doubled in bulk (after about forty minutes), add the remaining ingredients while mixing with a bread hook.

Set dough in a large pan, and allow to rise in a warm, draft-free place until doubled in bulk. Then punch down; allow to rise again till doubled; punch down once more. Now form the dough into loaves. Place them in well-oiled pans. Let loaves rise in pans for about twenty-five minutes or until they are fifty percent higher. Bake in a preheated 350°F oven for about one hour.

Peasant Black Bread

Yield – 10 to 12 loaves, 2¼ pounds each

6 tablespoons dry yeast
17 cups lukewarm coffee
3 cups blackstrap molasses
4 cups cornmeal
12 cups whole-wheat flour
6 cups burnt bread crumbs, toasted until dark brown
5 tablespoons salt
2 cups oil
4 cups rye flour
1 cup caraway seeds
12 cups unbleached white flour
More whole-wheat flour as needed

To make the sponge, combine the first five ingredients in a mixing bowl and put in a warm, draft-free place. When doubled in bulk (after about forty minutes), add the remaining ingredients while mixing with a bread hook. Set dough in a large pan and allow to rise in a warm place until doubled in bulk. Then punch down; allow to rise again till doubled; punch down once more. Now form the dough into loaves. This bread is particularly appealing if shaped into rounds. Oil the trays and dust with cornmeal or use baker's paper. Let loaves rise on trays for about twenty-five minutes. Bake in a preheated 350°F oven for forty minutes, brush with egg wash (two beaten egg whites mixed with four tablespoons water), then bake an additional twenty minutes.

Raisin Oatmeal Bread

Yield – 10 to 12 loaves, 2¼ pounds each

8 cups rolled oats
17 cups boiling water
6 tablespoons dry yeast
3 cups molasses
20 cups whole-wheat flour
5 tablespoons salt
3 cups melted butter
6 cups raisins
6 tablespoons cinnamon
More whole-wheat flour as needed (20 - 30 cups)

Soak rolled oats in boiling water and allow to cool to lukewarm. Then combine with yeast, molasses, and twenty cups whole-wheat flour to form a sponge. Let it rise in a warm place for about thirty minutes until doubled. Add the remaining ingredients while mixing with a bread hook. Set dough in a large pan and allow to rise in a warm, draft-free place until doubled in bulk. Then punch down; allow to rise again till doubled; punch down once more. Now form the dough into loaves. Place them in well-oiled pans. Let loaves rise in pans for about twenty-five minutes or until they are fifty percent higher. Bake in a preheated 350°F oven for about one hour.

Sesame Tahini Bread

Yield – 10 to 12 loaves, 2¼ pounds each

3 cups lukewarm water
6 tablespoons dry yeast
3 tablespoons honey or other sweetener
14 cups lukewarm water
3 cups honey
24 cups whole-wheat flour
5 tablespoons salt
4 cups sesame seeds
3 cups tahini
12 cups whole-wheat flour
More whole-wheat flour as needed (12 - 24 cups)

To proof the yeast, combine the first three ingredients in a mixing bowl. When the yeast foams, add the next four ingredients to make a sponge. Let it rise in a warm, draft-free place until doubled — thirty to forty minutes. Add the remaining ingredients slowly while mixing with a bread hook. Set dough in a large pan and allow to rise in a warm, draft-free place until doubled in bulk. Then punch down; allow to rise again till doubled; punch down once more. Now form the dough into loaves. Place them in well-oiled pans. Let loaves rise in pans for about twenty-five minutes or until they are fifty percent higher. Bake in a preheated 350°F oven for about one hour.

Swedish Limpa Rye Bread

Yield – 10 to 12 loaves, 2¼ pounds each

6 tablespoons dry yeast
17 cups lukewarm coffee
3 cups light molasses
16 cups whole-wheat flour
10 cups rye flour
5 tablespoons salt
2 cups oil
4 tablespoons fennel
4 tablespoons anise
4 tablespoons grated orange rind
16 cups unbleached white flour
More whole-wheat flour as needed

To make the sponge, combine the first five ingredients in a mixing bowl and place in a warm, draft-free place. When doubled in bulk (about forty minutes), add the remaining ingredients while mixing with a bread hook. Set dough in a large pan and allow to rise in a warm place until doubled in bulk. Then punch down; allow to rise again till doubled; punch down once more. Now form the dough into loaves. This bread is appealing if shaped into rounds. Oil the trays and dust with cornmeal or use baker's paper. Let loaves rise on trays for about twenty-five minutes. Bake in a pre heated 350°F oven for forty minutes, brush with egg wash (two beaten egg whites mixed with four tablespoons water), then bake an additional twenty minutes.

English Muffin Bread

Yield – 7 loaves, 2½ pounds each

6 tablespoons yeast
1 cup honey
5 cups warm water
9 cups warm milk
14 cups whole-wheat flour
12 cups unbleached white flour
4 tablespoons salt
1 tablespoon baking soda
2/3 cup warm milk

Combine flours and salt and set aside. Warm the milk. To proof the yeast, combine first three ingredients. When yeast foams, place it in a mixer and add flour mixture alternately with the nine cups of warm milk, stirring vigorously. Beat until it shows some elasticity and starts to leave the sides of the bowl. It will, however, remain rather loose and sticky. Cover and allow to rise for one hour. Now stir it down. Dissolve soda in two-thirds cup of milk and add to the dough. Beat rapidly for two full minutes. Spread dough in long, well-oiled loaf pans — fill no more than halfway. Let rise for one hour, then bake in a preheated 350°F oven until golden brown. To serve, slice and toast. This is a much easier way than making individual English muffins.

Tofu Dill Bread

Yield – 7 loaves, 2½ pounds each

1/2 cup yeast
4 cups warm water
1/2 cup honey
8 eggs, beaten
8 cups tofu, squeezed dry
1/2 cup minced onion
8 tablespoons dried or fresh dill weed
3 tablespoons salt
2 tablespoons black pepper
10 - 15 cups whole-wheat flour
10 - 15 cups unbleached white flour
More whole-wheat flour as needed

Proof yeast in water and honey in a mixing bowl. Add remaining ingredients and knead well using a bread hook. The dough should be slightly sticky. Allow to rise twice, then form into long loaves, plain or braided. Let loaves rise in pans for half an hour or till doubled in bulk. Bake at 375°F till golden brown, about forty-five minutes. Cottage cheese may be used in place of tofu.

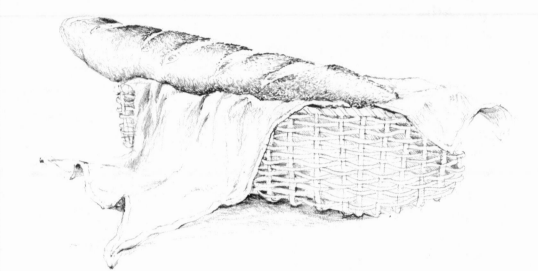

French/Italian Bread

Yield – 10 loaves, 2 pounds each

7 tablespoons yeast
3 cups lukewarm potato water*
3 tablespoons sweetener
12 cups lukewarm potato water*
24 cups whole-wheat flour
5 tablespoons salt
2 cups oil
16 cups unbleached white flour

Proof yeast by combining first three ingredients. When foamed, add potato water and whole-wheat flour. Let this sponge rise for twenty minutes, then add remaining ingredients. Adjust with enough whole-wheat flour to bring dough to proper consistency. Let it rise twice, then form into long loaves of two pounds each. Place on oiled sheet pans sprinkled with cornmeal, slash tops of loaves, and allow to rise for half an hour. Bake in a preheated 350°F oven for about forty-five minutes.

*Potato water is water that has been used to boil potatoes. If we cook potatoes to mash or for home fries, we save the water to use in bread. It adds flavor and helps the bread rise.

Arabian Flat Bread

Yield – (24 ten-inch rounds)

8 cups warm water
6 tablespoons yeast
1/2 cup honey
8 cups whole-wheat flour
2 cups melted butter
5 tablespoons salt
2 cups sesame seeds
12 - 16 cups whole-wheat flour

Make a sponge with the first four ingredients. Let it rise till doubled and bubbled, then add remaining ingredients. Allow to rise once. Divide into rounds the size of tennis balls. Roll each one out to a quarter-inch thickness. Brush with egg white and sprinkle with sesame seeds. Bake on ungreased cookie sheets at 350°F for twenty minutes or till golden. This makes a crispy cracker-bread, great with hummus.

Doughnuts

Yield – 60

8 tablespoons yeast
2 tablespoons honey
3 cups lukewarm water
1 cup warm water
4 eggs, beaten
2/3 cup oil
1 cup milk powder
8 cups whole-wheat flour
6 cups white flour
2/3 cup honey

To proof the yeast, combine it with two tablespoons honey and three cups of warm water. When foamed, combine with remaining ingredients. Let rise one and a half hours, then roll out into slabs three-quarters of an inch thick. Cut into doughnut shapes and allow to rise for forty-five minutes. Then deep-fry in 375°F oil till golden. Glaze with a mixture of honey or maple syrup mixed with arrowroot or cornstarch.

Unleavened Breads

Unleavened Cereal Bread

Yield	4	6	8	12	(3 pound loaves)
Cooked oatmeal	8	12	16	24	cups
Oil	½	¾	1	1½	cups
Sweetener	1	1½	2	3	cups
Salt	1	1½	2	3	tablespoons
Apple juice	2	3	4	5	cups
Whole-wheat flour	24	36	48	72	cups

Break up cooked oatmeal or other leftover cereal in mixer with a bread hook. Add the rest of the ingredients, saving the flour till last. Add flour slowly until the dough balls up — it should resemble heavy bread dough but be stickier. Add the flour while kneading, till earlobe consistency is reached. Shape into three-pound loaves. Place in well-oiled pans and allow to rise for twelve hours. Bake in a slow 325°F oven for two to three hours. Cool thoroughly, then slice very thin, preferably with a slicer. Most cereals work perfectly for this recipe. The amount of flour, salt, sweetener, and liquid all will vary slightly depending on the variety of cereal you use.

Unleavened Sweet Brown Rice Bread

Yield – 7 loaves, 3 pounds each

5 cups sweet brown rice
15 cups water
2 tablespoons salt
1 cup oil
1 cup sweetener
40 cups whole-wheat flour

Pressure-cook rice in salted water at fifteen pounds pressure for thirty minutes. Cool and place in mixer. Then add remaining ingredients, kneading well. Add flour only till it reaches earlobe consistency. Form into three-pound loaves and let rise for twelve hours. Bake in a 325°F oven for two to three hours. Allow to cool, then slice thin.

Basic Crackers

Yield – 2½ pounds

2 cups whole-wheat flour
5 cups oatmeal, freshly ground if possible
2 cups water
1 cup oil
2 teaspoons salt
1 cup sesame seeds

Combine water with oil till it turns milky. Mix the dry ingredients into the wet and knead till stiff. Roll out until thin, then brush with oil and sprinkle with salt. Cut into desired shapes. Place on cookie sheets and bake in a preheated 350°F oven for about twenty minutes or until golden brown.

Scones

Yield – (12-inch rounds)	2	4	8	16	
Servings	16	32	64	128	
Whole-wheat pastry flour	6	12	24	48	cups
Cream of tartar	1	2	4	8	tablespoons
Salt	1	2	4	8	teaspoons
Honey	1	2	4	8	tablespoons
Date bits or raisins	½	1	2	4	cups
Sour cream	1	2	4	8	cups

Mix the dry ingredients, then work in the sour cream until a stiff dough is formed. Break into equal parts according to the above chart. Roll each piece out into a twelve-inch round about half an inch thick. Fry on a dry, medium-hot grill until golden brown on both sides. Place in a 300°F oven until all rounds have been grilled, then cut each round into eight wedges to serve.

Tortillas

Yield – (4-inch rounds)	30	60	90	120	
Cornmeal	2	4	6	8	cups
Boiling water	3	6	9	12	cups
Salt	1	2	3	4	tablespoons
Butter	½	1	1½	2	cups
Whole-wheat flour	2	3	5	7	cups
Masa Harina corn flour*	2	4	5	7	cups
Unbleached white flour	2	3	5	7	cups

Whisk the cornmeal into the boiling water, stir in the salt and butter, and allow to simmer on a very low heat for ten minutes. Allow to cool for half an hour, then add remaining ingredients while kneading with a bread hook. Adjust with more or less flour to make a soft dough. Form into rounds the size of golf balls, then press into thin, flat, four-inch rounds. Use either a tortilla press or rolling pin and dust with Masa Harina corn flour while rolling out. Fry both sides on a hot, dry grill until brown or flecked with dark spots.

*Masa Harina is available at most large grocery stores. It is a fine cornmeal that has been ground with lime. There are several brands on the market.

3. Quick breads

Basic Biscuit

Yield	25	50	75	100	biscuits
Pastry flour	6	12	18	24	cups
Salt	2	4	5	6	teaspoons
Baking powder	3	6	9	12	tablespoons
Butter	½	1	1½	2	pounds
Milk	2½	5	7½	10	cups

Mix salt, flour, and baking powder. Cut in the butter. Add milk and stir as you pour. Adjust consistency with additional flour or milk to make a workable dough. Roll out until half an inch thick, cut into two-and-a-half-inch rounds, and bake in a 400°F oven for about twenty minutes or till done.

Advanced Biscuit

Yield	25	50	75	100	biscuits
Pastry flour	4	8	12	16	cups
Baking powder	2	4	6	8	tablespoons
Salt	1½	3	4½	6	teaspoons
Butter	5	10	15	20	tablespoons
Cornmeal	½	1	1½	2	cups
Wheat germ	½	1	1½	2	cups
Milk powder	½	1	1½	2	cups
Eggs	2	4	6	8	
Milk	1	2	3	4	cups
Additional milk	½	1	1½	2	cups

Mix flour, baking powder, and salt. Cut in the butter, then add the remaining dry ingredients. Mix eggs with the milk and add to flour mixture. Adjust with the additional milk to achieve a workable but dry dough. Roll out to a thickness of half an inch on a floured board, then cut into two-inch rounds. Bake on baker's paper or oiled cookie sheets. Pack them close together for soft biscuits, further apart for a crusty version. Bake in a preheated 400°F oven for fifteen to twenty minutes.

Basic Corn Bread

Servings	15	30	60	90	120	
Trays (11- x 14- x 2-inch)	1	2	4	6	8	
Whole-wheat flour	2½	5	10	15	20	cups
Cornmeal	2½	5	10	15	20	cups
Brown sugar	½	1	2	3	4	cups
Baking powder	2	4	8	12	16	tablespoons
Salt	½	1	2	3	4	tablespoons
Powdered milk	1	2	4	6	8	cups
Eggs, beaten	3	6	12	18	24	
Melted butter	½	1	2	3	4	cups
Water	1	2	4	6	8	quarts

Mix dry ingredients in a large bowl. Separately mix together the wet ones. Combine the two. This works out best when mixed by hand in a large bowl, adding wet to dry ingredients. If you grind the cornmeal yourself, set the mill to a grind slightly coarser than for flour. Pour into trays well-buttered or coated with *Lecithin Oil Mix*. Let stand thirty minutes, then bake in a preheated 400°F oven for thirty-five minutes or till golden brown. Top should spring back when lightly touched. For variation, try adding diced green and red peppers to the batter and dust with cumin and/or chili powder just before baking.

Custard Corn Bread

Servings	15	30	60	90	120	
Trays (11- x 14- x 2-inch)	1	2	4	6	8	
Cornmeal	2	4	8	12	16	cups
Whole-wheat flour	1	2	4	6	8	cups
White flour	½	1	2	3	4	cups
Baking powder	1½	3	6	9	12	tablespoons
Salt	½	1	2	3	4	tablespoons
Eggs, beaten	2	4	8	12	16	
Oil	½	1	2	3	4	cups
Honey	½	1	2	3	4	cups
Molasses	¼	½	1	1½	2	cups
Milk	5	10	20	30	40	cups

Mix dry ingredients in a large bowl. Combine wet ingredients in a separate one. Now mix the two together. This works best when mixed by hand in a large bowl, adding wet to dry ingredients. If you grind the cornmeal yourself, set the mill to a grind slightly coarser than for flour. It must be cornmeal, not corn flour, for this recipe to work properly. A three-layer bread will result: The cornmeal sinks to the bottom, the bran floats to the top, and a custard layer forms in the middle. The batter will seem loose; don't worry! Pour into trays well-buttered or coated with *Lecithin Oil Mix*. Let stand thirty minutes, then bake in a preheated 350°F oven for fifty minutes or until golden brown. The top should spring back when lightly touched.

Basic Muffins

Yield	30	60	90	120	180	muffins
Pastry flour	6	12	18	24	36	cups
Powdered milk	1	2	3	4	6	cups
Baking powder	1½	3	4½	6	9	tablespoons
Salt	½	1	1½	2	3	tablespoons
Eggs, beaten	5	10	15	20	30	
Oil	¾	1½	2	3	4	cups
Sour cream	1	2	3	4	6	cups
Yogurt	1	2	3	4	6	cups
Honey	1	2	3	4	6	cups

Mix the dry ingredients together in a large mixing bowl. In a separate bowl, blend the wet. Make a well in the flour mixture, add the wet ingredients, and stir carefully just till smooth. Use a whisk to gently break up any large clumps. Adjust consistency with liquid to obtain a spoonable dough. Grease the muffin tins with *Lecithin Oil Mix* and don't forget the tops of the tins. Fill the muffin wells two-thirds full and bake for twenty minutes or so at 375°F. For variation, replace up to half the volume with alternatives like rice flour or cornmeal. Add chopped nuts, date pieces, blueberries, cranberries and orange bits, or chopped apples. Or use maple syrup or molasses in place of honey.

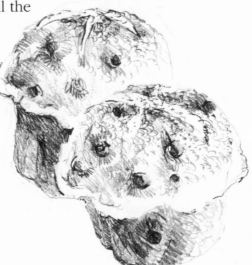

Corn Muffins

Yield – 24 muffins

2 cups whole-wheat pastry flour
2 cups cornmeal
1 teaspoon salt
2 tablespoons baking powder
2 cups milk or water
1/2 cup corn oil
1/2 cup barley malt

Sift dry ingredients together. Combine the liquids. Add wet to dry and mix gently. Use *Lecithin Oil Mix* on muffin tins, fill two-thirds full, and bake at 375°F for twenty minutes or until done.

Cranberry Muffins

Yield – 30 muffins

3/4 cup soy margarine
2½ cups sweetener (honey or maple syrup)
6 eggs
2½ cups orange juice
8 cups whole-wheat bread flour
1 tablespoon baking powder
1 tablespoon baking soda
2 teaspoons salt
2 cups chopped nuts
1 pound cranberries

Cream shortening and honey, then beat in eggs and juice. In a separate bowl, stir together all the dry ingredients (except cranberries and nuts). Combine the two mixtures and blend well. Fold in cranberries and nuts. Bake at 350°F for thirty-five minutes in well-greased muffin tins.

Coffee Cake

Servings	15	30	60	90	120	
Trays (11- x 14- x 2-inch)	1	2	4	6	8	
Whole-wheat pastry flour	5	10	20	30	40	cups
Baking powder	2	4	8	12	16	tablespoons
Salt	½	1	2	3	4	tablespoons
Brown sugar	½	1	2	3	4	cups
Maple syrup or honey	½	1	2	3	4	cups
Butter or soy margarine	¾	1½	3	4½	6	cups
Milk	1½	3	6	9	12	cups
Eggs	6	12	18	24	36	

Topping

	15	30	60	90	120	
Butter, melted	¼	½	1	1½	2	pounds
Brown sugar	½	1	2	3	4	cups
Walnuts, chopped	2	4	8	12	16	cups
Whole-wheat pastry flour	2	4	8	12	16	tablespoons
Cinnamon	2	4	8	12	16	tablespoons

Cream butter, then add sweeteners and eggs. Combine dry ingredients in a separate bowl, then add alternately with milk to the creamed mixture. Do not overbeat. Spread in well-greased trays. Mix topping ingredients together and sprinkle evenly on the batter. Bake at 350°F for forty minutes or until golden brown. Top should spring back when lightly touched.

Classic Raisin Bread from Scotland

Yield	2	4	8	12	16	loaves
Eggs	2	4	8	12	16	
Brown sugar	1	2	4	6	8	cups
Sour milk	2	4	8	12	16	cups
Molasses	½	1	2	3	4	cups
Whole-wheat flour	3	6	12	18	24	cups
Salt	1	2	4	6	8	teaspoons
Baking powder	1	2	4	6	8	teaspoons
Baking soda	2	4	8	12	16	teaspoons
Rolled oats	1½	3	6	9	12	cups
Walnuts, chopped	1	2	4	6	8	cups
Raisins	1	2	4	6	8	cups

Beat eggs, then add sugar, gradually beating well. Mix in the soured milk and molasses. Milk can be soured by adding one tablespoon of vinegar or lemon juice per cup. Sift together the flour, salt, baking powder, and baking soda. Combine with oats, nuts, and raisins, then add to the wet mixture, stirring only enough to combine. Divide dough in half, place in greased, (8- x 4- x 4-inch), paper-lined loaf pans. Bake in a preheated 350°F oven for one hour or till done. Each loaf should yield sixteen slices.

Sweet Rolls

Yield – 12 loaves, 2½ pounds each

7 tablespoons yeast
3 cups lukewarm coffee
3 tablespoons honey or maple syrup
10 cups lukewarm coffee
4 cups honey or maple syrup
24 eggs, beaten
20 cups whole-wheat pastry flour
8 cups white flour
6 tablespoons salt
2 cups oil
20 cups whole-wheat flour
10 - 20 cups white flour to finish dough

To proof the yeast, combine the first three ingredients in a mixing bowl. When the yeast foams, add the next four ingredients to make a sponge. Let rise until doubled, then add the remaining ingredients while mixing with a bread hook. Use enough flour to make a workable yet soft dough. Allow dough to rise twice, forty minutes each rise, then divide into twelve two-and-a-half-pound pieces. Knead into rounds, then roll out into large flats. Drizzle with melted butter and sweeteners, and sprinkle with any of the following: raisins, nutmeg, cinnamon, sliced almonds, walnuts, dates, poppy seeds, fresh or dried fruit pieces, sesame seeds. Carefully roll up into long loaves. Bake in a preheated 350°F oven for about one hour.

4. Pancakes, crepes and pie crusts

DON'T BE DUPED into thinking that using commercial pancake mixes is easier than making batter from scratch! If you follow some simple rules, the pancakes you make will be far superior in taste and nutrition to any packaged product. Always use freshly ground whole-grain flours. Separate the eggs and reserve stiffly beaten whites to fold in last. Mix batter just enough to blend the ingredients. When using a mixer, add dry to wet, but when mixing by hand, add wet to dry. Keep your batter on the thin side, and use a medium-hot, well-buttered grill. Always warm up your grill for thirty to forty minutes. Don't flip pancakes until they are covered with bubbles.

Hot, Buttered Orange Molasses

This is a great alternative to the traditional maple syrup.
Yield – 2 quarts

1/2 pound butter
1 cup frozen orange juice concentrate
6 cups light molasses
2 teaspoons cinnamon

Heat all ingredients over a slow flame in a heavy pot.

Bert's Lights :

Whole-Wheat Pastry Flour Pancakes

Servings	15	30	60	90	120	
Pastry flour	12	24	48	72	96	cups
Baking powder	¼	½	1	1½	2	cups
Salt	1	2	3	5	7	tablespoons
Milk powder	3	6	12	18	24	cups
Eggs	5	10	20	30	40	
Oil	½	1	2	3	4	cups
Honey	¼	½	1	1½	2	cups
Water	2	4	8	12	16	quarts

Combine dry ingredients and set aside. Separate eggs; beat whites till stiff and set aside. Combine wet and dry mixtures, adding dry to wet if using a power mixer, wet to dry if mixing by hand. Adjust consistency with more flour or water. Fold in the egg whites gently. Fry five-inch cakes on a well-buttered, medium- to high-heat grill. Most people expect whole-wheat pancakes to be heavy and soggy — not so in this case! Be prepared for the lightest, most delicious pancakes you have ever tasted.

Buckwheat Pancakes

Servings	15	30	60	90	120	
Pastry flour	6	12	24	36	48	cups
Buckwheat flour	6	12	24	36	48	cups
Baking powder	¼	½	1	1½	2	cups
Salt	1	2	3	5	6	tablespoons
Milk powder	1½	3	6	9	12	cups
Eggs	5	10	20	30	40	
Oil	½	1	2	3	4	cups
Molasses	¼	½	1	1½	2	cups
Water	2	4	8	12	16	quarts

Follow directions for the previous recipe.

Crowd-Pleaser Pancakes

Servings	15	30	60	90	120	
Whole-wheat bread flour	4	8	16	24	32	cups
Unbleached white flour	4	8	16	24	32	cups
Cornmeal	2	4	8	12	16	cups
Buckwheat flour	1½	3	6	9	12	cups
Baking powder	¼	½	1	1½	2	cups
Salt	1	2	3	5	6	tablespoons
Milk powder	1½	3	6	9	12	cups
Eggs	5	10	20	30	40	
Oil	½	1	2	3	4	cups
Honey	¼	½	1	1½	2	cups
Water	2	4	8	12	16	quarts

Follow the directions for *Bert's Lights*.

Hope's Crepes

Yield – 45 rounds, 6 inches in diameter

12 eggs
4 cups whole-wheat pastry flour
4 cups milk
1 cup water

Beat eggs. Sift in the flour and beat until smooth. Whisk in milk and water. Melt butter in a crepe pan. Pour in enough batter to coat the bottom of the pan thinly. Tilt pan while holding it over the heat to distribute the batter evenly. When the top of the crepe bubbles and begins to appear dry, flip it or turn it over with a spatula. Cook another minute or so, till light brown. Stack crepes until time to serve. Crepes can be filled with fancy fare such as crab or shrimp newburg, creamed vegetables, or ratatouille. They can also be stuffed with a dessert topping such as yogurt, sour cream, ricotta, and/or cottage cheese sweetened with honey or maple syrup, flavored with cinnamon, nutmeg, or vanilla. Top with fresh fruit after baking. Bake stuffed crepes till heated through, then top as desired. The original Italian version of manicotti is not pasta but crepes stuffed with ricotta cheese and spices, topped with oil and garlic or tomato sauce.

Basic Pie Crust

Trays (11- x 14- x 2-inch)	1	2	4	6	8	(bottom crusts)
Whole-wheat pastry flour	5	10	20	30	40	cups
Butter or soy margarine	½	1	2	3	4	pounds
Lemon juice	¼	½	1	1½	2	tablespoons
Cold water	¾	1½	3	4	5	cups

Cut butter into flour by hand or with a pastry-cutting attachment on a power mixer. When small beads form, sprinkle in the lemon juice and then the water until a proper pie dough consistency is reached. The important thing to remember is not to knead the dough any more than is necessary. Overkneading makes a tough crust. Divide into one-and-a-half-pound pieces and roll out between two sheets of plastic wrap. Prebake the crusts in a 375°F oven until light golden brown.

Mixed-Grain Pie Crust

Trays (11- x 14- x 2-inch)	1	2	4	6	8	(bottom crusts)
Whole-wheat pastry flour	2	4	8	12	16	cups
Oat flour	2	4	8	12	16	cups
Barley flour	½	1	2	3	4	cups
Oil, corn or peanut	½	1	2	3	4	cups
Salt	½	1	2	3	4	teaspoons
Cold water	1	2	3	4	6	cups

Mix all ingredients with a fork or pastry-cutting blade, slowly adding cold water until a workable pie dough is reached.

5. Soups

MY FIRST RESTAURANT, which featured a soup and bread menu, was where I discovered the versatility of the soup, salad, and bread lunch. Inventiveness and the use of available ingredients are the keys. Keep things simple. Many cooks think they have the option, if not the duty, to put everything into a soup but the proverbial kitchen sink. I recommend working with single flavors, as in squash soup. However, there is certainly room for a good stew or two in one's repertoire. Mix flavors carefully.

Broth is the foundation. The flavor and character of a soup are defined by its broth. The key to making a successful broth is having enough material to start with and enough time. Start with a clear idea of the soup you wish to serve. First, calculate how much soup will be needed for your group of diners. About five quarts of soup yield fifteen ten-ounce servings.

Join me for a moment, and let's make corn chowder for sixty people. How much do we need in all? Twenty quarts. Now we'll consider the proportions and quantities of the main ingredients. I'd suggest thirty-five percent cubed potatoes, twenty-five percent corn (whole and/or creamed), thirty percent milk, and ten percent diced celery and onions. Next we'll find the right size pot for twenty quarts of chowder: A thirty-quart pot will be perfect because the extra ten quarts allow for room to adjust the consistency, if necessary, by adding milk or corn.

Eight quarts of cubed potatoes will be about right. I cover them with water and cook them till just tender. Meanwhile, I sauté the diced onions and celery in butter. When the potatoes are tender, I toss them in and add six quarts of corn. Then I add about six to seven quarts of milk, whole and evaporated, and spoon through the chowder to check the consistency.

Seasoning is a very slow, cautious, and continuous process. By the time my soup is ready to serve, I have tasted it half a dozen times. (Use a tasting bowl and a wooden spoon — a metal spoon will burn your mouth.) Add salt and tamari with great care. Anticipate the point of no return before it happens! When choosing herbs and spices, keep simplicity in mind.

Note: When gauging the necessary quantity of soup for a large group, my rule of thumb is to make five to six quarts for every fifteen people. Less is required at lunchtime when served with bread, salad, fruit, and possibly cheese or tofu; more if it is a main-meal dish.

Corn Chowder for 60

8 quarts cubed potatoes - water to cover
2 (#10) cans of whole corn
4 cups diced onions

2 cups chopped celery
1 cup butter for sauté
5 quarts milk plus 1 quart evaporated milk
Season with salt, pepper, and a touch of tarragon

Basic Miso Soup

Sauté vegetables of your choice. I'd suggest including onions, garlic, and diced root vegetables. When the vegetables are just done, cover them with enough water to double the volume. Bring to a low boil and cook for about twenty minutes. Add about one teaspoon of miso paste per cup of soup. In order to avoid lumps, dissolve the miso in a little hot broth before adding it to the soup. Season with tamari and/or pepper. Miso itself is very salty, so add tamari with care. For richer, more substantial soups, add cooked grains and/or beans. Don't allow it to boil once the miso has been added: Too high a temperature kills the active enzymes present in miso. Just as the French and English rely on meat broth as a base for most of their soups, so I rely on miso broth. Plain miso broth is a wonderful alternative to afternoon tea or coffee.

Basic Miso Soup for 30

6 tablespoons safflower oil - for sauté
1 pound hatcho miso
1 tablespoon toasted sesame oil
1 pound onions, slivered
1/2 pound carrots, diced
1 head broccoli, diced
2 cloves garlic
2 teaspoons black pepper
10 quarts water
Tamari to taste
Serve with diced scallions

Minestrone

Start with a vegetable/miso broth, add crushed or whole tomatoes and cooked beans (such as chickpeas or white beans). Season generously with lots of garlic, parsley, oregano, basil, and freshly ground black pepper. Adding pasta is a traditional and nutritious option. Serve with grated parmesan cheese.

Minestrone for 30

10 quarts vegetable broth (or use Basic Miso Soup)
5 quarts canned tomatoes or leftover spaghetti sauce
1 quart cooked white beans or chickpeas
2 quarts cooked shells or other pasta
4 cloves garlic
1 cup chopped fresh parsley
Season with basil, oregano, black pepper, tamari
Serve with parmesan cheese

Split Pea Soup

Sauté diced onions, carrots, and garlic. Add dry split peas and water in a one-to-five ratio. (Use one quart of dry split peas with five quarts of water for every fifteen people.) Season to taste with tamari, black pepper, tarragon, and bay leaves. Bring to a boil and simmer for three to four hours till soup is thick and smooth. For complementary protein, serve with corn bread.

Split Pea Soup for 30

6 tablespoons oil
2 pounds onions, diced
1 pound carrots, diced
4 cloves garlic
2 quarts split peas
10 quarts water
1/2 cup tamari
2 teaspoons black pepper
1 bay leaf
1 tablespoon tarragon

Black Bean Soup

Cook black beans till tender, then mash by hand. Add enough vegetable stock or miso broth to make a thick soup. Sauté onions and garlic in oil ("hot" chili oil is optional), and add to the beans. Season with bay leaves, salt, pepper, and summer savory. Simmer for several hours. Serve topped with thin lemon slices.

Black Bean Soup for 30

2 quarts black beans cooked in 6 quarts water
3 quarts vegetable broth
1 quart spicy salsa
4 cloves garlic
1 cup tamari

Seaweed Soups

Cook seaweed as directed. Add a simple selection of sautéed vegetables, garlic, cooked grains, or pasta, if desired. Season with tamari, pepper — possibly miso. When you have leftover seaweed with broth, and aduki beans, just mix, heat, and serve. Be selective in what you choose to include in a seaweed soup — too many disparate items can create a "garbage" effect.

Seaweed Soup for 30

Follow directions for *Basic Miso Soup* and add 1 quart cooked seaweed.

6. Real food
for main meals

*Cooking Beans
and Other Legumes*

Pick through the legumes first to remove mud clumps, stones, and any that are off-color. Soak overnight in cold water. The next day, drain and cover with water. (See the following chart for ratios of water to beans.) Bring to a boil and simmer at a low boil for the times indicated. I usually cook beans with onion, garlic, and freshly ground black pepper. A touch of molasses enhances the flavor of certain varieties — particularly pinto and kidney.

Pressure-cooking circumvents the extremely long cooking times required by some legumes. Add salt or tamari *after* the beans are fully cooked to preserve tenderness. Leftover beans and broth make great soups and gravies.

110

Cooking Legumes

Variety	Ratio: water to dry beans	Time (hours)
Aduki beans	2½ : 1	1½
Black beans	3 : 1	4
Garbanzos (chickpeas)	3 : 1	4
Green lentil	2½ : 1	1½
Lima beans	2½ : 1	2
Mung beans	2½ : 1	2
Navy beans	2½ : 1	3
Red kidney beans	3 : 1	4
Red lentils	2½ : 1	1
Pinto beans	3 : 1	4
Soybeans	4 : 1	9
Split peas (for soup)	5 : 1	1½

Pressure-Cooked Beans

Variety	Ratio: water to dry beans		Time at 15 psi	
Soybeans	3	: 1	2	hours
Pinto beans	2½	: 1	25	minutes
Kidney beans	2½	: 1	25	minutes
Split peas - soup	4½	: 1	30	minutes
Chickpeas	2½	: 1	1	hour
Black beans	2 ½	: 1	1	hour

Timing always starts when fifteen pounds per square inch (15 psi) pressure has been reached. Make sure not to overfill your pressure cooker. Usually your pot should be no more than two-thirds full to allow space for a good head of pressure to build up. If your cooker doesn't have a dial pressure gauge, consult your instruction manual, because certain types of legumes — black beans, for example — *can* clog the steam vent. Large volumes of pressurized steam can be dangerous if not handled properly. Take the time to read the instruction book for your own pressure cooker.

Mexican Refried Beans

Yield – 50 servings

1 gallon pinto or black beans
1 pound onions, diced
1/2 pound green peppers, diced
3 cloves garlic, crushed
1/2 cup butter or oil
Salt, pepper, and cumin to taste

Cook the beans till very soft. Strain, reserving the juice. In a heavy skillet, sauté sliced onions, garlic, and green peppers in oil and/or butter. When they are well coated with oil and starting to sizzle, add the strained, cooked beans. Mash until a smooth, creamy bean paste has formed. Allow this to cook over a low flame for at least half an hour. Add cooking juice if beans get too dry. Season with salt, pepper, and cumin. Add grated cheddar if you wish. Refried beans go well with rice, or at breakfast with eggs and salsa — but, best of all, with tortillas.

Chili con Seitan

Yield – 75 servings

12 cups (dry measure) pinto and/or kidney beans
1 #10 can crushed tomatoes
2 #10 cans whole tomatoes
4 pounds onions, diced
2 pounds green peppers
3 pounds carrots, grated
2 pounds mushrooms, chunked
6 cloves garlic, crushed
6 tablespoons cumin
1½ cups Hot Oil
Adjust with broth (miso or vegetable)
Chili powder and cumin to taste
Salt and pepper to taste

Start with dried pinto beans, alone or in combination with kidney beans. Pressure-cook or simmer till done, according to the charts on the previous pages. In *Hot Oil*, sauté onions, garlic, green peppers, grated carrots, and mushrooms till just tender. Add to the cooked beans, along with crushed and whole tomatoes and miso or vegetable stock, until the proper consistency is reached. Season with chili, cumin, black pepper, and salt. For a vegetarian chili con carne, chunks of fried tofu or seitan can be added.

Vegetarian Pork and Beans

Servings	20	40	60	80	
Navy beans (dry)	1	2	3	4	quarts
Ketchup	½	1	1½	2	cups
Worcestershire sauce	1	2	3	4	tablespoons
Tamari	2	4	6	8	tablespoons
Dry mustard	1	2	3	4	teaspoons
Molasses	½	1	1½	2	cups
Honey	¼	½	¾	1	cup
Oil	1	2	3	4	tablespoons
Onions, diced	1	2	3	4	pounds
Garlic, crushed (cloves)	1	2	3	4	
Black pepper	1	2	3	4	teaspoons
Tofu, 3/4-inch cubes	1	2	3	4	pounds

Soak beans overnight using two and a half quarts of water for every quart of dry beans. In the morning, strain, place beans in a pot on top of the stove with just enough water to cover, bring to a boil, and simmer for thirty minutes. Meanwhile, sauté the cubed tofu till golden brown. Place beans in a covered baking tray or other bean pot, and add the tofu along with the remaining ingredients. Bake in a 325°F oven for eight to ten hours. Check after four hours, adding water if beans seem dry but not yet soft. You can't buy beans this tasty in a can.

Note: One quart of dry beans yields the same amount as four dollars worth of canned beans for a cost of only eighty cents.

Cooking Seaweeds

Soak seaweed in cold water till no more water is being absorbed, less than half an hour for most varieties. Drain. Meanwhile, sauté a few onion, garlic, and carrot slivers till tender. Add seaweed to sautéed vegetables and cover with water. Bring to a boil and simmer until the seaweed is tender, thirty minutes or so. Season with tamari, pepper, and fresh ginger if desired. Let it sit for half an hour to allow the flavors to blend. Use some of the cooking broth to keep seaweed moist and warm at the table, and serve sprinkled with freshly chopped chives or parsley for a striking black and green color combination.

Leftover seaweed and broth make a perfect base for the next day's soup. Leftover seaweed can also be marinated in an herbed oil and vinegar dressing for a cold sea-vegetable salad. Soaked seaweed can be added to soups for extra flavor and nutrition.

Baking Whole Foods

Baking is the simplest cooking method of all. It preserves the nutrients, liberates the top of your stove, and requires minimal preparation time.

Baked Vegetables

Certain vegetables are tastier baked rather than steamed or sautéed. On the other hand, some vegetables, like broccoli, do not take to baking because they are much too sensitive. Be selective and, as always, keep it simple. If you fill an 11- x 14- x 2-inch tray to the brim with carrot, parsnip, or beet chunks, it will serve twenty-five people or so. Leftovers are useful, too. The very best carrot/parsnip soup is made from vegetables baked till just brown in color. Cut the vegetable of choice into chunks — size and shape can be creatively manipulated. Remember that smaller pieces will cook through faster than larger ones. Don't use salt before baking. It leaches the moisture out of the vegetables.

Baked Squash

Squash does not necessarily have to be peeled — and some varieties are impossible to peel. I usually cut acorn squash into six or eight wedges, removing the seeds and basting with oil or butter before baking. Most types of squash should be baked at 375°F for forty-five to ninety minutes. This moderately high heat brings out the natural sweetness. Butternut squash should be scrubbed, peeled, cut into semicircles three-quarters of an inch thick, and brushed with a little sesame oil. Bake for forty-five minutes at 375°F with a little water in the bottom of a covered tray.

Baked Beets

Beets can be blanched and skinned before baking, but it's not really necessary. I suggest you simply wash them, cut them into wedges, scatter red onion slices on top, baste with garlic oil, and sprinkle with black pepper. Then cover with foil and poke several small holes in the foil to allow excess steam to escape. Baked beets are sweet and tender after one to one and a quarter hours at 375°F. Serve with a dollop of soy mayonnaise or sour cream and a sprinkle of fresh parsley. One full 11- x 14- x 2-inch tray yields thirty servings.

Baked Fish

If you are fortunate enough to have fresh fish available, I suggest baking it in a hot 400°F oven until it just starts to flake, fifteen to twenty minutes. We often use haddock fillets about three-quarters of an inch thick. Place the fish in oiled trays, baste with a mixture of garlic and melted butter, and season with black pepper. Timing depends on your ovens and the type of fish — but one signal is the smell. When the aroma of cooking fish fills the kitchen, it's probably overdone! The best fish chowder is made by baking whole fish for several hours. Clean and gut, of course, but leave head intact.

Baked Chicken

An "integrated" menu includes some meat. Chicken is the least expensive. We serve it once every seven to ten days. One 12- x 20- x 4-inch "hotel" tray will hold ten pounds of cut chicken nicely and will serve fifteen people — sparingly as far as they are concerned. I often sprinkle chicken with sesame seeds or black pepper, or baste it with a red barbecue sauce before the last forty-five minutes of cooking. Allow a good one and a half hours at 350 - 375°F to cook chicken thoroughly.

Sautéing Vegetables

If you learn how to do it properly, this basic cooking method will become one of your favorites. Buy local vegetables in season whenever possible. In winter months that often means little other than root vegetables and squash, but, if skillfully prepared, that is enough. Do not try to combine all the vegetables known to man in a single dish, just because they happen to be available. Keep it simple. I recommend starting with thinly sliced onions and crushed garlic, then adding up to three or four vegetables, prepared as indicated.

Broccoli	*- slice stalks thin, break up flowers*
Cauliflower	*- slice or break flowers*
Summer squash	*- slice into thin semicircles*
Butternut squash	*- slice in thin wedges*
Cabbage	*- shred or slice as desired*
Green or red peppers	*- cut into strips*
Mushrooms	*- slice or cut into chunks*
Peapods	*- whole*
Carrots	*- slice into thin circles*
Celery	*- slice on an angle*
Sprouts	*- toss in at the end and cook very briefly*

Cover the bottom of a skillet or wok with oil — the amount necessary depends upon the quantity of vegetables that you plan to cook. A rule of thumb is to start with one cup of oil for every 25 people that you are cooking for. Add more while sautéing if the pan gets too dry. I recommend using a thirty-inch wok, but a standard 20- x 12- x 4-inch hotel tray will also work. One tray will hold enough for thirty people. Start with crushed garlic and thinly sliced onions and sauté over a medium-high heat till they begin to sizzle. Then sauté vegetables one at a time, adding each new variety when the previous one begins to sizzle. Start with heavier types such as broccoli stalks or root vegetables, then proceed to vegetables such as celery or summer squash, followed by lighter species such as cabbage or mushrooms. Sprouts should be added last. The idea is to have all the vegetables perfectly cooked at the same time, just done but not mushy. Colors should be vivid and the texture crisp yet tender. With a bit of practice, you will learn when to add which vegetable, and have a feeling for the sizes and shapes that work best.

For a change of pace, try adding a few drops of *Hot Oil* to the basic sautéing oil. Let color guide your decision as to which vegetables to combine. An example of an attractive and tasty dish would be garlic, red and white onions, broccoli, red pepper slices, and mushrooms. You might also add a touch of curry or fresh ginger to the oil. Try an Italian-style sauté of onions, broccoli, cauliflower, mushrooms, and red tomato wedges (cooked last and least), seasoned with oregano, basil, and garlic.

When you are preparing more servings than your wok can accommodate, steam vegetables like broccoli and cauliflower buds while you sauté the delicate items such as onions, peppers, and mushrooms. When a wok is filled to the brim, the vegetables usually do not get cooked evenly. Add steamed items toward the end so that they may pick up the flavor of the oils and spices. A dash of toasted sesame oil, tossed in at the last moment, lends a marvelous flavor — don't miss it!

7. Main dishes

Spanakopita

This is a delightful casserole of Greek origin.

Servings	15	30	60	90	120	
Trays (11- x 14- x 2-inch)	1	2	4	6	8	
Spinach	2	4	8	12	16	pounds
Eggs, beaten	8	16	32	48	64	
Feta cheese, crumbled	1	2	4	6	8	pounds
Butter	¾	1½	3	4½	6	pounds
Filo dough	1	2	4	6	8	pounds
Mushrooms	½	1	1½	3	4	pounds
Onion, diced	1	2	4	6	8	pounds

Clean spinach and steam lightly. Meanwhile, mix eggs with feta cheese and season with black pepper. I suggest mixing the eggs and cheese for each tray in individual bowls rather than mixing them together. This way each tray gets its share. Melt the butter and set aside. Sauté mushrooms and diced onion in oil until just tender.

Now you are ready for the final assembly. Each pound of filo dough has about two dozen sheets. Butter the bottom of each tray. Carefully peel apart the filo dough, one sheet at a time, and arrange them in overlapping layers to cover the bottom of each tray, buttering each leaf as you go. This bottom crust will take ten to twelve sheets per tray — reserve about eight sheets for each top crust. Spread the steamed spinach and sautéed vegetables over the dough and pour in the beaten egg and feta cheese mixture. Cover with

the remaining sheets of filo dough, overlapping and buttering as before. Make several small knife slits in the top layer to allow steam to escape. Bake at 350°F for one and a quarter hours. Serve with ramen noodles, a green vegetable, and a salad garnished with black olives.

Vegetable Tempura Batter

Servings	15	30	60	90	120	
Eggs, beaten	8	16	32	48	64	
Arrowroot	1	2	3	4	6	cups
Cold water	5	10	20	30	40	cups
Salt	1	2	3	4	5	teaspoons
Whole-wheat pastry flour	5	10	20	30	40	cups
Sweet brown rice flour	3	6	12	18	24	cups

Blend the arrowroot powder in a small amount of the water, then mix with the remaining ingredients. Prepare this batter several hours ahead of time and chill it. Adjust consistency just before use by adding flour or water. The batter should be thick enough to coat each item without clumping up. The consistency of heavy cream is about right.

For vegetable tempura, dip vegetables in batter and fry in hot (375°F) oil until a crispy crust forms. The intense heat brings out the sweetness of most vegetables, particularly squashes and root vegetables such as parsnips and carrots. The quality of the oil you use makes or breaks this dish. At Hurricane Island we have one fryolator, so I can only cook enough for fifteen people at a time. I usually transfer the cooked vegetables to a warm oven (275°F) while I cook more, although tempura is best fresh from the oil. Keep them in the warming oven no longer than necessary.

Serve with a dipping sauce of tamari, water, ginger, and garlic. Appropriate vegetables for tempura include mushrooms cut in quarters and halves; onions and peppers sliced into rings; cauliflower and broccoli flowers with some stem left on; carrots and other root vegetables cut into thin circles or matchsticks; and butternut squash cut into quarter-inch-thick wedges or strips. For dessert, tempura apple wedges or banana circles drizzled with honey or maple syrup are delicious.

Mystery Meat (Seitan)

Yield – 24 servings

32 cups whole-wheat flour
12 cups water

This is a wonderful meat substitute! I have passed this off as meat many times; most people won't know if you don't tell. Sometimes it is called "wheat meat."

In a power mixer, combine whole-wheat flour with water. Work it well till a dough forms, then knead until very stiff. This can be done by hand if no dough mixer is available. The object is to develop the gluten as in making bread. Place the bowl of seitan dough in a sink and cover the dough with warm water. Start squeezing it through your fingers, allowing the starch to dissolve in the water. Keep squeezing until you have a very milky liquid and a loose dough. Pour out the milky water and cover dough with fresh cold water. This will pull the gluten together, making the dough very stringy. Again discard the water and cover it this time with warm water. Keep squeezing.

Alternate from warm to cold until little or no starch clouds the water. It should take about five rounds. Finally, slice the stringy mass into cutlets, place in a pot and cover with boiling water. Season with one and a half cups of tamari, fresh garlic, and ginger. Simmer for forty-five minutes. After cooking, strain and squeeze out excess water. Cut the seitan into chunks or strips and fry till brown before using in stews or chili. Or serve like steak with grain, vegetable, and gravy. It also makes a good sandwich filler — try a seitan reuben!

Tofu

Yield – 8 pounds

1½ gallons soybeans
3½ gallons water
7 gallons water
curdling agent (2 cups lemon juice or 1/4 cup nigari)

Because commercial tofu is now so readily available in this country, it is no longer essential to make it yourself. But if you want to try, here is my method. I am fortunate to live near the ocean, which provides salt water, a good curdling agent. However, lemon juice or nigari may be used with reasonable results.

Soak soybeans in three and a half gallons of water overnight. The next morning, put two forty-quart pots on a high heat to boil, each with three and a half gallons of water. Meanwhile, strain the beans and blend them with an equal amount of hot water. Divide the bean slur or "goo" (as the Japanese say) between the two pots of boiling water. Bring to a foamy boil, and then strain through fine cheesecloth. The resulting liquid is soy milk (see page 153).

The residual bean pulp is called "okara," and can be used in soy burgers or added to bread dough. You should have a total of ten gallons of soy milk. Set two gallons aside for other purposes and heat the remaining eight gallons to a rolling boil in a forty-quart pot. It takes a while to bring that much milk to a boil, so remember to stir it to prevent it from scorching.

After it has boiled for a full five minutes, remove from heat and add enough curdling agent to form curds in a relatively clear whey. Now, carefully ladle off the whey without disturbing the curds — they are quite fragile. Gently place the curds in a tofu pressing-box and press two hours. Remove from the box, cover with cold water, and refrigerate. Change the water every other day, and use within four to five days. For more detailed information, I would suggest reading *The Book of Tofu*. See bibliography.

Tofu – Baked, Sautéed, or Fried

Use 1 pound of tofu for every 6 people

To bake, slice tofu cakes into slabs half an inch thick. Baste with garlic oil, and season with fresh black pepper, salt or tamari. Sprinkle with nutritional yeast, if desired. Bake on oiled cookie sheets in a 375°F oven till golden brown. To sauté or deep fry, cut into cubes an inch thick and fry till golden. Tofu is also good when dipped in tempura batter before frying. Remember, it's bland — serve it with tamari, sesame salt, or other condiments.

Soysage Burgers

Yield – 60 patties

16 cups okara (soybean pulp)
8 cups whole-wheat pastry flour
1½ cups nutritional yeast flakes
1 cup oil
3/4 cup tamari
2 tablespoons salt
2 tablespoons black pepper
1 cup sesame tahini
1 teaspoon each sage, rosemary, and thyme
Optional ingredients: grated cheese, eggs, hot sauce, minced onions

Blend all ingredients in a mixer, using a dough hook. Add extra flour as needed to make a workable consistency. Form patties and place on oiled cookie sheets. Bake in a 350°F oven for forty-five minutes or till golden brown. Serve with lettuce, tomato slices, onion, mustard, and ketchup on whole-wheat bread or rolls.

Tofu Salad or Mock Egg Salad

Yield – 20 servings

1 pound tofu, mashed
3 cups soy mayonnaise
1 pound diced celery
1/2 pound diced red onion
1/2 pound diced green and/or red pepper
1 pound tofu cut into half-inch cubes

Combine tofu with soy mayonnaise; add celery, onion, and peppers.
Fold in tofu cubes. Season with salt, black pepper, dry mustard, or curry
powder. Serve on a bed of lettuce or in sandwiches.

Tempeh - Baked or Sautéed

One eight-ounce package of tempeh provides enough protein for four
to five servings. I usually serve it with a grain, vegetables, and sauce or
gravy. To bake, baste generously with garlic oil, season with salt and
pepper, cut into small squares (ten pieces per eight-ounce package) and
bake at 375°F till dark, golden brown — about forty-five minutes. To
sauté, cut into smaller pieces or slivers. It soaks up a lot of oil, so don't
be surprised. I recommend sautéing the tempeh first by itself, then
sautéing the vegetables, then combining them at the last minute.

Mexican Pie

Servings	5	30	60	90	120	
Trays (11- x 14- x 2-inch)	1	2	4	6	8	
Cornmeal	2	4	8	12	16	cups
Water (for cornmeal)	5	10	20	30	40	cups
Butter	¼	½	1	1½	2	pounds
Salt	2	4	8	12	16	teaspoons
Tomato sauce	1	2	4	6	8	quarts
Pinto beans (dry)	2	4	8	12	16	cups
Grated cheese	½	1	2	3	4	pounds

Bring water to a boil, place in the top of a double boiler, and whisk in the cornmeal. Cook till thick, about twenty minutes, and then add butter and salt. Spread the cornmeal mush into well-buttered trays and bake at 350°F till firm, about thirty minutes. Meanwhile, cook the beans till soft — pressure-cooking is the best method (see page 112). Then make the *Refried Beans* (page 112). Next, sauté enough vegetables to cover the cornmeal mush in each tray. I suggest trying onions, broccoli, and mushrooms. Whole-kernel corn may be used in place of, or combined with vegetables. Make a traditional tomato spaghetti sauce, but season with cumin and chili oil instead of the herbs usually associated with spaghetti sauce. When cornmeal is done, spread with a layer each of refried beans, sautéed vegetables and/or whole- kernel corn, and spicy tomato sauce. Sprinkle the top with grated cheese. Bake at 350°F for one hour. Serve with a green salad and a cooked vegetable.

Baked Stuffed Lasagna

Servings	15	30	60	90	120	
Trays (11- x 14- x 2-inch)	1	2	4	6	8	
Eggs - beaten	3	6	10	15	20	
Ricotta cheese	3	6	12	18	24	pounds
Parmesan cheese	1	2	4	6	8	cups
Salt	1	2	4	6	8	teaspoons
Black pepper	½	1	2	3	4	tablespoons
Garlic, oregano, basil			(to taste)			
Fresh pasta	1	2	4	6	8	pounds
Mozzarella cheese	1	2	4	6	8	pounds
Spaghetti sauce	1½	3	6	9	12	quarts

Combine eggs, ricotta, parmesan, salt, and pepper. Season with garlic, oregano, and basil. Cut mozzarella into slices an eighth of an inch thick and set aside. Cook the lasagna noodles in boiling water, stirring gently without breaking the strips. When just tender, drain and rinse in cold water.

Oil each tray and cover with a layer of noodles, then a layer of mozzarella slices. Spread with half of the cheese and egg mixture, then a thin layer of tomato sauce. Cover with another layer of noodles, more mozzarella, the remainder of the cheese and egg mixture, and another thin layer of sauce. Top with a final layer each of noodles and tomato sauce. Bake at 350°F for one hour and ten minutes.

Eggplant Parmesan

Servings	15	30	60	90	120	
Trays (11- x 14- x 2-inch)	1	2	4	6	8	
Eggplant	2½	5	10	15	20	pounds
Mozzarella cheese	1	2	4	6	8	pounds
Parmesan cheese	1	2	4	6	8	cups
Bread crumbs	½	1	2	3	4	cups
Spaghetti sauce	1	2	4	6	8	quarts
Eggs	8	16	32	48	64	

Peel eggplant and slice lengthwise; it will shrink when fried, so slices should be at least half an inch thick. Baste with garlic oil and fry on a grill or in a skillet until tender. Season with salt and pepper while cooking.

Arrange layers of cooked eggplant on the bottom of each tray and sprinkle with bread crumbs and plenty of parmesan cheese. Beat four eggs per tray and pour on. Next cover each tray with slices of mozzarella cheese an eighth of an inch thick. Then add a second layer each of cooked eggplant, parmesan cheese, and bread crumbs. Beat the remaining eggs and divide equally among the trays. Cover with a second layer of mozzarella slices and top with spaghetti sauce. Bake at 350°F for one hour. Serve with Italian bread, salad, a vegetable, and a side dish of artichoke spaghetti.

Ratatouille

Servings	15	30	60	90	120	
Oil	1	2	3	4	5	cups
Onions, minced	1½	3	6	9	12	pounds
Garlic, crushed (cloves)	3	6	9	12	16	
Green pepper wedges	½	1	2	3	4	pounds
Celery, diced	½	1	2	3	4	pounds
Eggplant, 1-inch cubes	2	4	8	12	16	pounds
Zucchini squash, cubed	1	2	4	6	8	pounds
Mushrooms, quartered	½	1	2	3	4	pounds
Whole tomatoes	1	2	4	6	8	#10 cans
Oregano	½	1	2	3	4	tablespoons
Basil	½	1	2	3	4	tablespoons

Salt, pepper, and tamari to taste

Sauté onions and garlic in oil till transparent. Add cut fresh vegetables in the order listed. Sauté till all are tender, then add the canned tomatoes and season with oregano, basil, tamari, salt, and pepper. Simmer slowly for four to five hours. Serve over rice or pasta, topped with grated parmesan cheese.

Quiche

Servings	15	30	60	90	120	
Trays (11- x 14- x 2-inch)	1	2	4	6	8	
Eggs, beaten	10	20	40	60	80	
Evaporated milk	2	4	8	12	16	cups
Whole milk	2	4	8	12	16	cups
Salt	1	2	4	6	8	teaspoons
Black pepper	¼	½	1	1½	2	teaspoons
Mushrooms, sliced	½	1	2	3	4	pounds
Onions, diced	½	1	2	3	4	pounds
Cheese, grated	1½	3	6	9	12	pounds

Combine eggs, milk, salt, and pepper in a large bowl. Line the bottom of each tray with pie crust (see page 102) and prebake until lightly golden. Sauté enough vegetables to cover the bottom of each tray. Mushrooms and onions are suggested above, but many other vegetables would work just as well.

Spread the vegetables over the crusts, sprinkle with grated cheese, and pour in the milk/egg mixture. Dust with cayenne pepper and nutmeg. Bake at 375°F till golden brown and firm. Serve with garden salad, baked bulgur, and a contrasting vegetable. This dish is very popular and offers a wide variety of options. Try using toasted seaweed strips or dulse instead of the traditional additions of bacon or ham.

Cheesy Noodle Casserole

Servings	15	30	60	90	120	
Trays (11- x 14- x 2-inch)	1	2	4	6	8	
Butter	½	1	2	3	4	pounds
Whole-wheat pastry flour	2	4	8	12	16	cups
Evaporated milk	2	4	8	12	16	cups
Whole milk	2	4	8	12	16	cups
Cheese, grated	1	2	4	6	8	pounds
Black pepper	¼	½	1	1½	2	teaspoons
Parmesan cheese, grated	½	1	2	3	4	cups
Tahini	1½	3	6	9	12	cups
Tamari	½	1	2	3	4	cups
Shells or elbow pasta	2	4	8	12	16	dry measure quarts

Make a roux of the butter and flour. Add milk and heat in a double boiler. Add the cheese, tahini, tamari, and pepper. Cook until the sauce starts to thicken. Meanwhile, boil shell or elbow noodles in salted water until just tender. Spread the cooked noodles in trays. Sprinkle, if desired, with sautéed vegetables. Cover with cheese sauce and sprinkle with sesame seeds. Bake at 350°F for one hour.

Pizza

It takes a lot of practice to make a one-hundred-percent whole-wheat pizza crust that will please the public. I recommend starting with this slightly lighter version.

Servings	15	30	60	90	120	
Trays (20 x 30-inch)	1	2	4	6	8	

The Dough

Dry yeast	1	2	4	6	8	tablespoons
Warm water	½	1	2	3	4	cups
Sweetener	1	2	4	6	8	tablespoons

Proof the yeast in water with sweetener until it foams, then add to the following:

Warm water	2	4	8	12	16	cups
Oil	½	1	2	3	4	cups
Salt	½	1	2	3	4	tablespoons
Whole-wheat flour	3	6	12	18	24	cups

Slowly add the white flour until a sticky dough is formed.

White flour	2	5	10	5	20	cups

Add more flour if needed

To proof the yeast, combine the first three ingredients. When foamy, add remaining warm water, oil, salt, and whole-wheat flour. Slowly incorporate the white flour until a sticky dough is formed. Knead using additional flour as needed to form a soft dough. Allow it to rise until doubled, punch down, rise again. Form into three-pound bread rounds, then roll out into 20- x 30-inch rectangles on a smooth board, dusting with whole-wheat pastry flour as you work. Place on oiled trays sprinkled with cornmeal. Let rise another twenty minutes, then place in preheated 350°F ovens until just barely cooked, about twenty minutes. Don't overcook them at this stage — they will be baked for another thirty-five minutes later on.

Dressing the Pizza

Servings	15	30	60	90	120	
Trays	1	2	4	6	8	
Grated cheese	1½	3	6	9	12	pounds
Sauce	2	4	8	12	16	quarts

Spread the prebaked crusts with pizza sauce — a thick, spicy tomato sauce. You will need about two quarts of sauce per tray. Cover with a mixture of grated cheese — eighty percent mozzarella, fifteen percent cheddar, five percent parmesan.

Sprinkle with black pepper, oregano, and basil. Top with a combination of ingredients — black olive slices, thinly sliced onions, mushrooms, and green peppers are my choices, but there are many delicious options. Try sliced tofu strips; broccoli spears; feta cheese and black olive slices; mushroom and avocado slices; seitan strips; crumbled, cooked tempeh; or seafoods such as shrimp or tuna. You can also use seasoned tofu instead of cheese. Bake the dressed pizza at 375°F for thirty-five minutes or till the cheese starts to bubble and the vegetables are properly cooked.

Kedgeree

Yield – 15 servings

Originally brought to us from India by the British, kedgeree is a simple combination of curried rice, hard-boiled eggs, and flaked, cooked white fish such as cod, haddock, or halibut. At Hurricane Island we serve this often. It is a very popular yet reasonably priced dish.

1/4 cup oil
2 onions (chopped)
2 cloves garlic (minced)
1 tablespoon curry powder
6 cups cooked brown rice
2 pounds cooked white fish (flaked)
4 hard-boiled eggs
black pepper to taste
fresh parsley (chopped)

Sauté onions, garlic, and curry powder in oil. When the onions are transparent, lower the heat and add the rice. When heated through, gently stir in the fish. Chop the hard-boiled eggs into eighths and add. Season with black pepper to taste and sprinkle with freshly chopped parsley. Tofu, fried until golden brown, can replace fish, eggs, or both. Serve for lunch with soup and salad.

8. Salads and dressings

SALADS ARE A GREAT WAY to increase the use of real foods and eliminate processed foods. Don't buy ready-made salads — they spoil very quickly. Preparing fresh salads requires minimal time and effort. One head of iceberg lettuce makes twelve servings, and a standard case of iceberg lettuce contains twenty-four heads. The basic salad on the next page only becomes "Italian" if you include the ingredients marked with an asterisk. One quart of a thick, creamy dressing makes twenty-five servings, while simple vinaigrette goes nearly twice as far.

Basic Italian Salad

Yield – 50 servings

5 heads iceberg lettuce, shredded by hand
6 tomatoes,* cut in wedges
5 green peppers, sliced in thin circles
1½ pounds red onions, sliced in thin circles
3 cups whole black olives,* not pitted
3 cucumbers, thinly sliced
1½ cups olive oil* with garlic (see page 140)
3 tablespoons oregano*
3 tablespoons basil*
1 tablespoon black pepper
salt to taste
1 cup red wine vinegar

Mix all the vegetables in a large bowl. As you toss the salad, sprinkle on the olive oil, using just enough to coat the leaves and make them shine. Some oils spread better than others, so the quantity needed will vary. Shake on the salt and pepper, and sprinkle with basil and oregano rubbed between your fingertips to bring out the flavor. Finally, sprinkle on the vinegar about ten minutes before serving time.

*These make it Italian.

Coleslaw

Servings	15	30	60	90	120	
Green cabbage	2½	5	10	15	20	pounds
Red cabbage	½	1	2	3	4	pounds
Carrots	1	2	4	6	8	pounds
Red onions	1	2	4	6	8	pounds
Raisins (optional)	½	1	2	3	4	pounds

Coleslaw Dressing

Servings	15	30	60	90	120	
Soy or egg mayonnaise	1½	3	6	8	12	cups
Dry mustard	1	2	4	6	8	teaspoons
Salt	1	2	4	6	8	teaspoons
Black pepper	2	4	6	8	10	teaspoons
Red wine vinegar	2	4	8	12	16	tablespoons
Honey	1	2	4	6	8	tablespoons

Slice onions and cabbage *very* thin. Grate carrots finely. Toss vegetables with raisins in a large bowl. In a separate bowl, combine the rest of the ingredients. Dress the coleslaw just before serving. To vary, try adding apple bits and/or nuts.

Tofu Salad Dressing

Yield – 1 quart (25-plus servings)

1½ cups safflower oil
1/2 cup sesame oil
1 cup juice of fresh lemons
4 cloves garlic, crushed
1½ pounds tofu
1 cup wine vinegar
4 tablespoons umeboshi plum paste
black pepper to taste

Blend all ingredients until smooth and creamy. Serve on dark-green leafy salads and try a garnish of toasted tempeh croutons! Pickled umeboshi plums are used extensively in Japanese and macrobiotic cooking. Whole plums and paste are readily available from health-food wholesalers. Their flavor is at once tart, salty, and sweet — adding an unusual touch to this dressing.

Orange Tahini Dressing

Yield – 1 quart (serves 35)

2 cups orange juice
2 fresh oranges, peeled and seeded
2 cups tahini
2 tablespoons honey
3 tablespoons tamari soy sauce
1 teaspoon black pepper

Blend all ingredients till smooth. Thicken with more tahini or thin with a touch of apple juice, if necessary.

Basic Vinaigrette Dressing

Yield – 6 cups (serves 50)

4 cups olive oil
2 cups lemon juice
1/2 cup herb or wine vinegar
1 tablespoon black pepper
2 teaspoons salt
4 cloves garlic, crushed
1 teaspoon dry mustard

Stir the mustard, salt, pepper, and garlic into some of the oil to form a paste. Add the remaining ingredients and blend well. For a richer, creamier dressing, add one egg for every cup of oil; for a sweeter dressing, try a touch of honey.

Soy Mayonnaise

Yield – 6 cups
(This recipe is for a one-gallon blender — adjust quantities to fit your blender.)

2 cups soy milk, cold (see page 153)
4 - 5 cups oil
4 tablespoons vinegar
3 teaspoons salt
1/2 teaspoon dry mustard
2 tablespoons honey
1 tablespoon black pepper
3 shakes Tabasco sauce

Place soy milk in blender. With blender on, slowly add the oil. When the mixture starts to form cavities (the sign that the oil is thick and saturated), stop the blender and remove the dressing. Add the remaining ingredients. For use in *Soy Frosting*, substitute a natural sweetener at this point (see page 155). Blend in a bowl with wire whisk, then refrigerate till needed.

Garlic Oil

Blend ten cloves freshly crushed garlic in four cups of olive (or other) oil. Store in the cooler and use for sautéing and salad dressings. Garlic powder (ugh) should only be used in dire emergencies.

Tabouli

Servings	15	30	60	90	120	
Bulgur	3	6	12	18	24	cups
Water	4	8	16	24	32	cups
Mint leaves	1	2	4	6	8	tablespoons
Salt	1	2	3	4	6	teaspoons
Olive oil	¼	½	1	1½	2	cups
Garlic, crushed	1	2	3	4	6	cloves
Fresh parsley, chopped	¼	½	1	1½	2	cups
Diced tomatoes	½	1	2	3	4	cups
Cucumber, diced	½	1	2	3	4	cups
Red onion, minced	¼	½	1	1½	2	cups
Lemon juice	½	1	2	3	4	cups

Use a covered pot over a low flame to cook the bulgur with mint leaves in salted water for about twenty minutes or until all the water is absorbed. Refrigerate overnight or till cool. Combine the vegetables, then dress with the remaining ingredients. You can make tabouli with leftover bulgur by simply adding fresh chopped mint and dressing as above; follow the quantities for the thirty-serving column for every twelve cups of cooked grain that you have. This makes a great summer luncheon dish.

9. Gravies and sauces

Yeast Gravy

Servings	15	30	60	90	120	
Nutritional yeast	½	1	2	3	4	cups
Whole-wheat pastry flour	½	1	2	3	4	cups
Oil	⅓	¾	1½	2	2½	cups
Tamari	¼	⅓	⅔	1	1¼	cups
Boiling water	2½	5	10	15	20	cups

This recipe works best if you use nutritional yeast as opposed to a debittered brewer's yeast. Toast the flour and yeast in a dry frying pan until it gives off a nutty aroma. Be careful not to let it burn. When lightly toasted, mix in the oil, coating all of the flour thoroughly. Whisk in half the water, then the tamari, and finally add the rest of the water slowly, whisking all the time. Simmer for twenty minutes. Add more water as necessary for a proper gravy consistency. Season with black pepper. This is a great addition to any grain-based meal. Don't miss this one.

Mushroom Gravy

Servings	15	30	60	90	120	
Onions, diced	1	2	4	6	8	cups
Mushrooms, sliced	½	1	2	3	4	pounds
Whole-wheat pastry flour	¾	1	3	4½	6	cups
Nutritional yeast	¼	½	1	1½	2	cups
Oil	½	1	1½	2¼	3	cups
Tamari	¼	½	1	1¼	2	cups
Boiling water	2½	5	10	15	20	cups

Dry-roast the flour and yeast in a skillet till golden brown. Meanwhile, sauté the onions and mushrooms in a heavy pot. When the mushrooms are just tender, lower the heat and stir in the toasted flour/yeast combination. Mix thoroughly. Add the tamari and water slowly, stirring well. Season with black pepper. Simmer for twenty minutes, adjusting consistency with water if too thick.

Bechamel Sauce

Servings	15	30	60	90	120	
Onions, diced	½	1	2	3	4	cups
Sesame oil	⅛	¼	½	¾	1	cup
Whole-wheat pastry flour	½	1	2	3	4	cups
Vegetable stock or water	2½	5	10	15	20	cups
Tamari	1	2	4	6	8	tablespoons

Sauté onions in oil till transparent. Stir in flour, coating it well with oil. Add water slowly, stirring with a whisk. Season with the tamari and pepper while simmering over a low flame. Add water if too thick. For a variation, try using half rice flour, half whole-wheat.

Miso Tahini Gravy

Servings	15	30	60	90	120	
Water, boiling	1	2	4	6	8	cups
Miso	½	1	2	3	4	cups
Tahini	½	1	2	3	4	cups
Tamari	½	1	2	3	4	tablespoons
Honey	½	1	2	3	4	teaspoons

Mix all ingredients, blending with a whisk until smooth. Vary the ratio of miso to tahini — additional miso makes a saltier sauce, while more tahini will give a sweeter one. Serve over sautéed vegetables, grains, and so on.

Creamy Oat Gravy

This is a great sauce for grains, beans, vegetables, or cabbage rolls, and also can be used as a soup base.

Servings	15	30	60	90	120	
Water	2½	5	10	15	20	cups
Oat flour	1	2	4	6	8	cups
Oil	⅛	¼	½	¾	1	cups
Onions, diced	½	1	2	3	4	pounds
Tamari	3	6	9	12	16	tablespoons
Garlic, crushed	2	4	5	6	8	cloves
Sage	1	2	4	6	8	tablespoons
Thyme	½	1	2	3	4	teaspoons
Black pepper	½	1	2	3	4	teaspoons

Dry-roast the oat flour in a frying pan until it gives off a nutty aroma. In a separate pot, sauté garlic and onions in oil, then stir in toasted flour, coating it well with oil. Add the rest of the ingredients and bring to a boil. Simmer for half an hour, stirring occasionally. Adjust consistency with vegetable stock or water before serving over grain and vegetables.

Brown Sauce

Yield – enough for 2 pounds of tofu or tempeh

1 cup water
1 tablespoon arrowroot powder, dissolved in some of the water
1/4 cup tamari
1 teaspoon toasted sesame oil
minced fresh ginger and garlic to taste

Both tempeh and tofu can be coated with the ubiquitous brown sauce that so many Oriental restaurants feature. This sauce is made right in the wok or frying pan containing the vegetables and tempeh or tofu. Use a dash of toasted sesame oil along with the minced garlic and ginger in the stir-fry. When tempeh or tofu is done, combine sauce ingredients and pour into fry pan. Over a medium heat it will thicken and coat everything. Seasonings can be varied from hot (chili) to sweet (honey) to sour (rice vinegar). This is a very versatile gravy.

Marcia's Hot and Spicy
Peanut Butter Sauce

Yield – 30 servings
An Indonesian favorite, this sauce is delicious on soba noodles, raw vegetables, or as a tempura dip. You may substitute tahini for the peanut butter as a variation. Serve hot or cold.

1 cup peanut butter
5 tablespoons tamari
3 tablespoons honey
6 tablespoons toasted sesame oil
3 tablespoons rice vinegar
3 tablespoons Hot Oil
1 cup hot water or vegetable broth
2 cloves garlic, crushed
2 tablespoons grated ginger

Combine all ingredients. Heat, whisking constantly, adding liquid as necessary to achieve a good gravy consistency. Serve hot, tossed with three pounds of soba noodles and topped with finely chopped scallions. Or use as a cold dressing for raw vegetables, as they do in Indonesia.

Oil and Garlic Sauce

Lightly sauté garlic in pure olive oil and/or butter and mix into cooked pasta. Season with salt and freshly ground black pepper. Top with grated parmesan cheese. If desired, add fresh mushrooms and/or fresh or canned baby clams. This is a very rich dish, but absolutely delicious.

Traditional Spaghetti Sauce

Although it is not a soup, I approach spaghetti sauce in much the same manner. Start with a good olive oil and sauté lots of garlic, onions, green peppers, and mushrooms in it. Then add whole and crushed tomatoes and season with basil, oregano, bay leaves, salt, and pepper. Simmer it all day. For an imaginative touch, try adding red wine, anise, fennel, or chili pepper.

Sour Cream and Butter Sauce for Fettucini

Servings	15	30	60	90	120	
Butter	½	1	2	3	4	pounds
Parmesan cheese	½	1	2	3	4	cups
Sour cream	1	2	3	4	6	pounds

Melt butter in a heavy saucepan. Whisk in grated parmesan cheese and sour cream. Season with lots of freshly ground pepper, basil, oregano, and fresh garlic. Serve over hot cooked fettucini, with an extra dollop of sauce on top. Sprinkle with freshly chopped parsley. If you have lost some of your fans with too much seaweed and rice, this will bring them back!

Some Like It Hot

Chili is the hottest spice available. Unfortunately, whole or dried chilies are difficult to cook because the pieces and seeds are unreasonably hot and hard to chew. If you use powdered chili you'll avoid these problems, but it is usually stale and weak by the time you buy it. Below are two ways to use dried chilies which allow you to control the hotness easily.

Hot Oil

Oriental grocery stores carry an item called "hot oil" that is perfect for adding a hot aftertaste to sautéed vegetables or other dishes. Unfortunately, it is expensive — but, fortunately, you can make it cheaply yourself. Blend half a cup of dried chilies with two cups of a high-grade oil. Sesame is wonderful, but any variety will do. When well blended, place in a heavy saucepan and simmer for three minutes. Allow it to cool and then strain it through a fine sieve. Use small amounts when sautéing when you desire a hot flavor in a soup or vegetable dish.

Hot Sauce

Simmer a half cup of dried chilies in three cups of water for fifteen minutes. Remove from heat, allow to cool, then blend till smooth. Don't breathe in the fumes. Strain through a sieve. To give you an idea of how potent this stuff is, dip the end of your finger in and put a drop on your tongue.

10. Spreads, dips, yogurt, alternative beverages

Spreads and Dips

Hummus

Yield – 100 servings

1 gallon chickpeas
2½ gallons water
1 cup olive oil
6 - 8 cups bean cooking stock
6 - 8 cups tahini
2 cups lemon juice
8 cloves garlic, crushed
2 tablespoons salt
2 tablespoons black pepper

Pressure-cook chickpeas in water at fifteen pounds pressure for one and a quarter hours. Strain, reserving the stock. Mash in a mixer, then add remaining ingredients. Mix well. Add more bean stock if too thick. It should have the consistency of a loose batter, and will thicken a bit as it cools. Serve with bread or crackers, sprouts, and red-onion wedges.

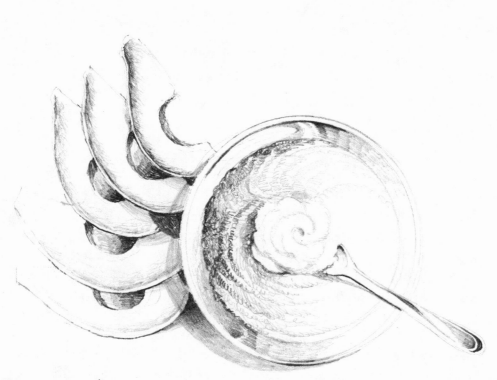

Guacamole

Yield – 30 servings

6 ripe avocados
juice of 1 lemon
3 teaspoons dry mustard
2 tablespoons ground cumin
1/2 cup yogurt or sour cream
2 tablespoons olive oil
1 tablespoon Tabasco or Hot Oil
4 cloves garlic, crushed
salt and pepper to taste

Peel and mash avocados. Blend in the remaining ingredients with a hand whisk. Serve with a Mexican meal (see pages 89 and 112).

Yogurt

Fresh Milk Yogurt

Yield – 2 gallons

12 cups plain yogurt
1½ gallons fresh milk
1 quart evaporated or instant powdered milk (optional)

Set plain yogurt out to warm up to room temperature. While this "starter" is warming up, heat fresh milk to scalding (180°F) Do not boil! When the milk reaches 180°F, remove from heat and allow to cool. This scalding process kills any undesirable bacteria present in the milk that might interfere with the growth of the yogurt culture. When the milk has cooled to lukewarm (110°F), gently stir in the yogurt starter. At this point, add evaporated or instant powdered milk, if desired, for a richer, creamier texture. The next step is to incubate the mixture. A gas oven with a pilot light works perfectly, although any draft-free place with an ambient temperature of 90-100°F will serve just as well. You may also wrap the vessel in a sleeping bag or use a thermos bottle. Incubation time is usually six to ten hours. The yogurt is ready to chill when it has set and has a heavy, creamlike consistency. Always reserve twelve cups of yogurt as a starter for the next batch.

Quick and Easy Yogurt

Yield – 3 gallons

2 gallons of lukewarm water
16 cups instant milk powder
4 (6-ounce) cans of evaporated milk (not condensed milk)
8 - 12 cups plain yogurt

Add the powdered milk to the water, mix well, then add the rest of the ingredients. Incubate as in the preceding yogurt recipe. This method bypasses the scalding process since powdered and evaporated milk are already sterilized.

Alternative Beverages

Soy Milk

Yield – 4 gallons

10 cups soybeans
24 cups cold water
hot water as needed
3½ gallons boiling water

Soak soybeans in cold water overnight. In the morning, strain. Pulverize small amounts of the beans in a blender with an equal amount of hot water. A one-gallon blender can comfortably process eight cups of soaked beans plus eight cups of water. Blend till you have a smooth slur. Add slur to boiling water in a large pot. Cook until it boils and foams up, then strain through cheesecloth. The resulting four gallons of white liquid is soy milk. Refrigerate till cool. Soy milk can be used in place of cow's milk in most recipes. To make a palatable drink, add honey and vanilla according to taste. For other uses see *Soy Mayonnaise* or *Soy Frosting*.

Hot Carob Drink

Servings	20	40	80	120	
Carob powder, roasted	2	4	8	12	cups
Boiling water	2	4	8	12	cups
Milk or soy milk	1	2	4	6	gallons
Vanilla	1	2	4	6	tablespoons
Honey	½	1	2	3	cups
Molasses	½	1	2	3	cups
Cinnamon	1	2	4	6	teaspoons
Nutmeg	1	2	4	6	teaspoons

Heat cow's milk or soy milk. Whisk the carob and boiling water together to make a slur and combine with some of the hot milk. Add to the rest of the milk and flavor with the remaining ingredients to taste. Try adding some coffee for a mocha flavor or orange extract and ice for a delightful cold carob drink.

11. Desserts

Basic Cake

Servings	15	30	60	90	120	
Trays (11- x 14- x 2-inch)	1	2	4	6	8	
Butter	½	1	2	3	4	pounds
Honey	½	1	2	3	4	cups
Brown sugar	1	2	4	6	8	cups
Soy flour	¼	½	1	1½	2	cups
Whole-wheat pastry flour	3	7	14	21	28	cups
Baking powder	1½	3	6	9	12	tablespoons
Salt	½	1	2	3	4	tablespoons
Milk	1½	3½	7	10	14	cups
Eggs	6	12	24	32	40	

Cream the butter, honey, sugar, and soy flour. Add eggs, a few at a time, and mix. Combine the flour, salt, and baking powder in a separate bowl, then add to the creamed mixture alternately with the milk. Do not over-

154

beat, as that tends to make a cake tough. Divide between well-greased trays and bake at 350°F till golden brown, about forty minutes. Top should spring back when lightly touched. Many variations are possible with this basic recipe. Try lining the bottom of trays with crushed pine-apple and a little honey to make pineapple upside-down cakes. Or substitute maple syrup for some of the honey and brown sugar and add walnuts to make maple-walnut cakes. Substitute coffee for half of the milk, and add four tablespoons of carob powder per tray, to make mocha cakes.

Soy Frosting

Follow the *Soy Mayonnaise* recipe to make a plain soy whip. In place of the herbs and spices, add honey or maple syrup to taste, and flavor with cinnamon, nutmeg, and vanilla. You can make any variety of frosting you desire with this basic recipe.

Carrot Cake

Servings	15	30	60	90	120	
Trays (11- x 14- x 2-inch)	1	2	4	6	8	
Carrots, grated	2½	5	10	15	20	cups
Sweetener	½	3	6	9	12	cups
Eggs, beaten	5	10	20	30	40	
Pastry flour	2½	5	10	15	20	cups
Oil	1	2	4	6	8	cups
Salt	1	2	4	6	8	teaspoons
Nutmeg	1	2	4	6	8	teaspoons
Baking soda	1	2	4	6	8	tablespoons
Cinnamon	1	2	4	6	8	tablespoons

Mix together the oil, sweetener, eggs, and carrots. Blend in the rest of the ingredients. Place in buttered trays and bake at 350°F for one hour. Honey or maple syrup makes good sweeteners.

Freddy's Zucchini Bread

Servings	15	30	60	90	120	
Trays (11- x 14- x 2-inch)	1	2	4	6	8	
Eggs, beaten	4	8	16	24	32	
Brown sugar	1½	3	6	9	12	cups
Oil	1½	3	6	9	12	cups
Zucchini, grated	3	6	12	18	24	cups
Vanilla	1	2	3	4	6	tablespoons
Juice and peels of . . .	1	2	3	4	6	oranges
Juice and peels of . . .	1	2	3	4	6	lemons
Whole-wheat pastry flour	5	10	20	30	40	cups
Salt	½	1	2	3	4	tablespoons
Baking soda	½	1	2	3	4	tablespoons
Baking powder	½	1	2	3	4	teaspoons
Cinnamon	½	1	2	3	4	tablespoons
Walnuts, chopped	1½	3	6	9	12	cups

Combine first seven ingredients and mix well. Then add remaining ingredients. Pour into buttered trays and bake for one hour at 350°F.

Baked Custard

Servings	15	30	60	90	120	
Trays (11- x 14- x 2-inch)	1	2	4	6	8	
Eggs, beaten	8	16	32	48	64	
Sweetener	1½	3	6	9	12	cups
Vanilla	1	2	3	4	6	teaspoons
Salt	1	2	3	4	5	teaspoons
Milk (soy or dairy)	2	4	8	12	16	quarts

Blend all ingredients and pour into trays well oiled with *Lecithin Oil Mix*. Sprinkle with nutmeg and cinnamon. Place trays in sheet pans half filled with water (or use another water-bath system). Bake in a slow oven at 325°F for two hours, or till set. For variation, replace some of the milk with coffee, or measure half a cup of carob powder per tray, combine with eggs, and proceed as directed above. Try combining both of the above options for a mocha custard.

Indian Pudding

Servings	15	30	60	90	120	
Trays (11- x 14x 2-inch)	1	2	4	6	8	
Milk	2½	5	10	15	20	quarts
Cornmeal	1½	3	6	9	12	cups
Melted butter	¼	½	1	1½	2	pounds
Molasses	1	2	4	6	8	cups
Honey	1	2	4	6	8	cups
Salt	1	1½	3	4	6	tablespoons
Cinnamon	1	1½	3	4	6	tablespoons
Ginger	1	2	4	6	8	teaspoons
Eggs	6	12	22	33	44	

Scald milk. Pour in the cornmeal, whisking steadily. Cook in a double boiler for twenty minutes till mixture thickens. Melt butter and combine with sweeteners, salt, ginger, and cinnamon. Beat eggs well. Now add both to the cornmeal mush and stir thoroughly. Pour into well-greased pans, bake in a water bath for several hours at 325°F. Test with a knife or toothpick. If knife or toothpick comes out clean, it is done.

Bread Pudding

Servings	15	30	60	90	120	
Trays (11- x 14- x 2-inch)	1	2	4	6	8	
Bread cubes (1/2-inch)	2	4	8	12	16	quarts
Raisins	1	2	4	6	8	cups
Eggs, beaten	6	12	24	36	48	
Milk	6	12	24	36	48	cups
Evaporated milk	2	4	8	12	16	cups
Honey or maple syrup	½	1	2	3	4	cups
Molasses	¼	½	1	1½	2	cups
Vanilla	1	2	3	4	6	tablespoons

Divide bread cubes evenly between oiled trays. Add the raisins. Combine remaining ingredients, then pour over the bread cubes. Sprinkle with nutmeg and cinnamon. Place trays in water baths and bake at 350°F for one hour, or until set. For variation, add carob powder, chopped apples, sweetened tofu, or dates. You may substitute leftover grains for bread cubes.

Oat Bars

Servings	15	30	60	90	120	
Trays (11- x 14- x 2-inch)	1	2	4	6	8	
Butter	1	2	4	6	8	cups
Brown sugar	1	2	4	6	8	cups
Honey	¾	1½	3	4½	6	cups
Eggs, beaten	2	4	8	12	16	
Vanilla	1	2	3	4	6	tablespoons
Whole-wheat pastry flour	2½	5	10	15	20	cups
Baking soda	½	1	2	3	4	tablespoons
Salt	¼	½	1	1½	2	tablespoons
Rolled oats	3	6	12	18	24	cups
Walnuts, chopped	1	2	4	6	8	cups
Raisins	1	2	4	6	8	cups

Cream the butter, sugar, and honey. Add eggs and vanilla. Combine the whole-wheat pastry flour with the baking soda and salt and add to the creamed mixture. Fold in the rolled oats, walnuts, and raisins. Pour evenly into well-greased, floured pans. Bake in a preheated 350°F oven for fifty minutes. Cut fifteen bars in each tray while still warm, but do not remove from pans until cool.

Scottish Shortbread Squares

Servings	15	30	60	90	120	
Trays (11- x 14- x 2-inch)	1	2	4	6	8	
Butter	1½	3	6	9	12	cups
Brown sugar	1½	3	6	9	12	cups
Rice flour	1½	3	6	9	12	cups
Whole-wheat pastry flour	4	8	16	24	32	cups
Vanilla		1	2	3	4	6	teaspoons
Salt		1	2	4	6	8	teaspoons

Cream the butter, sugar, and vanilla. In a separate bowl mix the dry ingredients together, then blend into the creamed mixture. Pat batter into trays. It should be half an inch thick. Bake in a 325°F oven for about forty-five minutes or until light, golden brown. Cut into squares while dough is still warm.

Solo Bars

Yield – 60 bars, 2 ounces each

2 pounds pitted dates
2 pounds figs (stems removed)
2 pounds raisins
2 cups cashew pieces
1 cup sesame seeds
2 cups peanut butter

Mix all ingredients except peanut butter and run through a meat grinder. Add peanut butter and knead in a mixer with a dough hook. Roll out into half-inch-thick sheets. Cut into two-ounce bars. These "solo bars" are standard issue for a Hurricane Island two- or three-day solo expedition. Usually, it is the only food a student will have other than the wild edibles available on the uninhabited island where he or she has been placed.

Carob and Honey Brownies

Servings	15	30	60	90	120	
Trays (11- x 14- x 2-inch)	1	2	4	6	8	
Butter	1	2	4	6	8	cups
Honey	1	2	4	6	8	cups
Eggs, beaten	4	8	16	24	32	
Vanilla	2	4	8	12	16	teaspoons
Salt	1	2	4	6	8	teaspoons
Carob powder	1	2	4	6	8	cups
Whole-wheat pastry flour	1½	3	6	9	12	cups
Baking powder	1	2	4	6	8	tablespoons
Walnuts, chopped	2	4	8	12	16	cups
Milk	¼	½	1	1½	2	cups

Cream butter, eggs, vanilla, salt, and honey. Sift the dry ingredients and
combine with the creamed mixture. Then add milk and nuts. Pat into
well-buttered trays and bake in a preheated 350°F oven for thirty minutes or until done. For variation, add raisins and/or carob chips.

Pound Cake

Yield – 6 loaves, 2 pounds each

4 pounds butter
10 cups brown sugar
1 teaspoon salt
24 eggs
4 cups milk
2 tablespoons vanilla
16 cups whole-wheat pastry flour
4 tablespoons baking powder

Cream first four ingredients. In a separate bowl, combine milk and
vanilla. In a third bowl, mix flour with baking powder. Now add the
wet and dry ingredients alternately to the creamed mixture. Spoon into
well-buttered pans until about two-thirds full. Bake in a 350°F oven for
just over one hour. Check centers with a knife blade or toothpick.

Granola Cookies

Yield	3	6	12	24	dozen
Safflower oil	¾	1½	3	6	cups
Honey	¾	1½	3	6	cups
Eggs, beaten	2	4	8	16	
Nuts, chopped	¾	1½	3	6	cups
Vanilla	1	2	4	8	teaspoons
Whole-wheat pastry flour	¾	1½	3	6	cups
Salt	½	1	2	4	teaspoons
Granola	2	4	8	16	cups
Raisins	½	1	2	4	cups
Cinnamon	1	2	4	8	teaspoons

Mix oil and honey. Add eggs, nuts, and vanilla, and beat well. Mix together the flour and salt, sift, and combine with the batter. Add the granola, raisins, and cinnamon. Drop by spoonfuls onto well-oiled cookie sheets. Bake twenty minutes or so in a 325°F oven.

Peanut Butter Cookies

Yield – 24, 3-inch diameter

1/2 pound butter
1/2 cup brown sugar
1/3 cup honey
1 egg
1 cup natural peanut butter
1/2 teaspoon salt
1/2 teaspoon baking soda
1½ cups whole-wheat pastry flour
1/2 teaspoon vanilla

Cream butter with sugar and honey. Beat in egg, peanut butter, salt, and soda. Lastly, blend in the flour and vanilla. Roll the dough into small balls and place on greased cookie sheets. Press flat with a fork and bake for about fifteen minutes at 375°F.

Peanut Butter Fudge

Yield – 14 pounds

12 pounds peanut butter
4 cups honey
3 cups powdered milk
3 cups raisins
3 cups carob chips

Mix all ingredients in a bread mixer with a dough hook. Roll out and cut into squares. One recipe makes a hundred and fifty pieces of one-and-a-half ounces each. This is an energy candy perfect for camping and hiking trips.

About Outward Bound

The Hurricane Island Outward Bound School is a nonprofit educational organization serving thousands of students in Maine, New Hampshire, New York, and Florida. Outward Bound's purpose is to address the educational development of the total person by conducting mentally and physically demanding courses in remote wilderness areas. Outward Bound believes that an individual develops self-reliance, concern for others, and leadership skills when confronted by challenging, shared experiences involving service and adventure. Its address is P.O. Box 429, Rockland, Maine 04841.

When I first started working with the Hurricane Island Outward Bound School I had little idea of what it really did. As time went on, I began to realize that Outward Bound is a physical metaphor for an inner journey that we all experience. It is a journey of confronting one's fears and working through those fears. It is a process of discovery of one's compassion and tolerance for others. It is about communication and leadership. It is about relating to one's self and others in a stressful situation. It is about voluntary simplicity in a natural environment. It works!

About the Author

Rick Perry was born in 1945 and raised in Reading, Massachusetts. He holds a degree from Berklee College of Music, Boston, in jazz composition, and was an active studio musician, playing both flute and saxophone, in the late 1960s. He also studied electrical engineering at Northeastern University for two years. Armed with this diverse background, he brought both art and science to the preparation and presentation of natural foods. In the early 1970s in Exeter, New Hampshire, he opened two restaurants, the Loaf and Ladle and the Spaghetti Kitchen, as well as a natural-foods store called the Green Earth. The restaurants are still in operation today. In the winter months Rick lives in Portland, Maine, where he is a free-lance photographer. His photographs have appeared in many books and publications about the Maine coast. From April through October he is to be found on Hurricane Island, off the coast of Rockland, Maine, where he has been the food service director for the Hurricane Island Outward Bound School since 1975.

Books of Interest

Aberera, Michael, *Cooking For Life*, New York, Avon, 1970.

Abrahamson, E.M., M.D., and Pezet, A.W., *Body, Mind & Sugar,* New York, Avon, 1951.

Brown, Edward, *Tassajara Bread Book* and *Tassajara Cooking,* Berkeley, Shambala, 1973.

Dufty, William, *Sugar Blues*, New York, Warner Books, 1975.

Friedlander, Barbara, *The Findhorn Cookbook*, New York, Grosset & Dunlap, 1976.

Kushi, Michio, *The Teachings of Michio Kushi*, Brookline, Mass., East West Foundation, 1972.

Lappé, Frances, *Diet for a Small Planet*, New York, Ballantine, 1971.

Miller, Saul, *Food for Thought*, Englewood Cliffs, New Jersey, Prentice-Hall, 1979.

Oshowa, Lima, *The Art of Just Cooking*, Brookline, Mass., Autumn Press, 1974.

Shurtleff, William, and Aoyagi, Akiko, *The Book of Tofu*, Brookline, Mass., Autumn Press, 1975.

Index

Anadama bread
(corn/molasses) 76
Arabian flat bread 85

Baked beets 116-117
Baked chicken 117
Baked custard 157
Baked fish 117
Baked grains 56-57
Baked orange millet 68
Baked squash 116
Baked whole foods 116
Baked vegetables 116
Beans (see Legumes)
Beans - Mexican refried 112
Beans - vegetarian pork and 114
Bechamel sauce 143
Beets - baked 116–117
Beverages 44-45
Biscuit
basic 90
advanced 91
Black bean soup 109
Blender 49
Bread
Arabian flat 85
basic 74, 75-76
cereal 88
corn and molasses
(anadama) 76
English muffin 82
French/Italian 84
millet 77
peasant black 78
raisin oatmeal 79

scones 88
Scottish raisin 96
sesame tahini 80
Swedish limpa rye 81
sweet rolls 97
tofu dill 83
unleavened cereal 86
unleavened sweet rice 87
yeast 73
zucchini 156
Bread pudding 158
Breakfast cereals 58-65
Brown rice - about 34, 57
Brown sauce 145
Brownies - carob honey 161
Buckwheat - about 31
Buckwheat pancakes 100

Cake
basic 154
carrot 155
coffee 95
pound 161
Carob drink 153
Carob honey brownies 161
Carrot cake 155
Casserole - cheesy noodle 131
Cereals - breakfast 58-65
Cheesy noodle casserole 131
Chicken - baked 117
Chili con seitan 113
Coffee 45
Coffee cake 95
Coleslaw 137-138

Cookies
    granola 162
    peanut butter 163
Corn - about 33
Corn and molasses bread 76
Corn bread
    basic 91
    custard 92
Corn chowder 105-106
Corn muffin 94
Corn oil 39
Cornmeal mush 65
Cornmeal - polenta 67
Cost-effectiveness 28
Crackers - basic 88
Cranberry muffin 94
Cream cereals 59
Crepes - Hope's 101
Crowd-pleaser pancakes 100
Custard - baked 157
Custard corn bread 92
Cutlery 50

Doughnuts 85
Dressing (see Salad dressing)

Eggplant parmesan 128
English muffin bread 82
Equipment 46

Familia 63
Fearn Natural Foods 73
Fettucini, sauce for 147
Fish - baked 117
Flour - about 35

Flour mill 48
Freezer 49
French/Italian bread 84
Frosting - soy 155
Fruit juice 44
Fryolator 50
Fudge - peanut butter 163

Garlic oil 140
Grain room setup 52-53
Grains 12
Grains
    baked 56–57
    pressure-cooking 57
Granola 64
Granola cookies 162
Gravy
    creamy oat 144
    miso tahini 144
    mushroom 143
    yeast 142
Guacamole 151

Hot buttered molasses 99
Hot carob drink 153
Hot oil 148
Hot peanut sauce 146
Hot sauce 148
Hummus 150

Indian pudding 157
Integration of natural foods 12
Irish oatmeal 60
Italian salad - basic 137
Italian bread 84

Kedgeree 134

Lasagna - noodles 68-71
    see Pasta
Lasagna - baked stuffed 127
Lecithin oil mix 73
Leftover management 30
Legumes
    about 37
    cooking 110-111
    pressure-cooking 112

Macrobiotic 10
Mayonnaise - soy 140
Meadows Mill Co. 48
Meat - red 40
Menu
    luncheon 22-25
    main meals 20-21
Mexican pie 126
Mexican refried beans 112
Mexican tortillas 89
Mill
    flour 48
    spice 50
Millet
    about 34
    baked orange 68
Millet bread 77
Minestrone 107
Miso soup 106
Miso tahini gravy 144
Mixer 49
Molasses - hot, buttered 99
Morning cereal 60

Muffin
    basic 93
    corn 94
    cranberry 94
Mushroom gravy 143

Noodle casserole - cheesy 131

Oat bars 158
Oat gravy 144
Oatmeal
    basic 63
    creamy 61
    familia 63
    granola 64
    hearty 62
    Irish 60
    Scotch 62
Oats - about 34
Oil
    about 38
    corn 39
    garlic 140
    hot 148
    lecithin mix 73
    olive 39
    peanut 39
    safflower 39
    sesame 39
    soy 39
    sunflower 39
Oil and garlic sauce 147
Olive oil 39
Orange tahini salad
    dressing 139

Pancakes 98
    buckwheat 100
    crowd-pleaser 100
    whole-wheat 99
Pasta
    handmade 68–69
    meals 19
    quantity 71
Peanut butter cookies 163
Peanut butter fudge 163
Peanut butter sauce - hot 146
Peanut oil 39
Peasant black bread 78
Pie - Mexican 126
Pie crusts
    basic 102
    mixed grain 103
Pizza 132-133
Polenta - corn 67
Potatoes - home-fried 66
Pound cake 161
Pressure-cooking grains 57
Pudding
    bread 158
    Indian 157

Quiche 130
Quinoa 34

Raisin bread - scottish 96
Raisin oatmeal bread 79
Ratatouille 129
Red meat 40
Refrigeration 49
Reuben - vegetarian 122

Rice cream 58
Rolls - sweet 97
Rye 33

Safflower oil 39
Salad
    basic Italian 137
    coleslaw 137-138
    tabouli 141
    tofu 125
Salad dressing
    basic Italian 137
    coleslaw 138
    orange tahini 139
    tofu 138
    vinaigrette 139
Salads 136–141
Sauce
    bechamel 143
    brown 145
    hot 148
    oil and garlic 147
    peanut butter - hot 146
    sour cream /butter 147
    spaghetti 147
Sautéed vegetables 118-119
Scones 86
Scotch oatmeal 62
Scottish shortbread 159
Scottish raisin bread 96
Sea vegetables 41
Seaweed
    about 41
    cooking 115
Seaweed soup 109

Seitan 122
Seitan - chili con 113
Serving 26
Sesame oil 39
Sesame tahini bread 80
Shortbread - Scottish 159
Slicer 49
Soft drinks 44
Solo bars 160
Soup
    black bean 109
    corn chowder 105-106
    minestrone 107
    miso 106
    seaweed 109
    split pea 108
Soy bean - about 36
Soy frosting 155
Soy mayonnaise 140
Soy milk 153
Soy oil 39
Soysage 124
Spaghetti sauce 147
Spanakopita 120
Spice mill 50
Spices 43
Split pea soup 108
Squash - baked 116
Staples 52-53
Steam table 49
Stove - commercial 47
Sunflower oil 39
Swedish limpa rye bread 81
Sweet rice bread -
    unleavened 87

Sweet rolls 97
Sweeteners 40

Tabouli 141
Tea 44-45
Tempeh
    about 36
    baked or sautéed 125
Tempura - vegetable 121
Time line for cooking 27
Tofu
    about 37
    cooking 124
    making 123
Tofu dill bread 83
Tofu salad 125
Tofu salad dressing 138
Tortillas - wheat and corn 89

Unleavened cereal bread 86
Unleavened sweet brown rice
    bread 87

Vegetable tempura 121
Vegetables
    baked 116
    sautéed 118-119
Vegetarian pork and beans 114
Vegetarian reuben 122
Vinaigrette salad dressing 139

Water 44
Wheat - about 32
Whole-wheat pancakes 99
Whole grains 12

Yeast bread 73
Yeast gravy 142
Yogurt
    about 42
    fresh milk 152
    quick 152

Zucchini bread 156

Acknowledgement

The following people have contributed to the completion of this book:

Marcia Howell, Libby Kesner, Claire Marno, Carol Marno,
Hope Marno, Peter Fisher, Bert Weiss, Sue Harvey, Peals Wrobel,
Bob Kellerman, Peter and Betty Willauer, William Rosenberg,
Walden and Kathleen Whitham, J. Christian Peterson,
Christine Stephanson, Carlos Freddy Morales, Alan Sterman,
John Kostandin, Tom Shellenberger, Mrs. Frank Lommano,
Gerald F. Rooney, and Craig Langford.

Thanks to Julia Ackerman for many hours of editing.